LAST-MINUTE KNITTED GIFTS

LAST-MINUTE

KNITTED GIFTS

JOELLE HOVERSON

PHOTOGRAPHS BY ANNA WILLIAMS

STC CRAFT | A MELANIE FALICK BOOK | NEW YORK

Editor: Melanie Falick

Designer: Asya Palatova
Production Director: Kim Tyner

Library of Congress Cataloging-in-Publication Data
Hoverson, Joelle. Last-minute knitted gifts / Joelle Hoverson ;
photographs by Anna Williams— 1st ed.
p. cm.
Includes index.
ISBN 1-58479-367-8 (hardcover)
1. Knitting—Patterns. 2. Gifts. I. Williams, Anna. II. Title.
TT825.H677 2004
746.43'2043—dc22
2004006111

Published in 2004 by
Stewart, Tabori & Chang
An imprint of Harry N. Abrams, Inc.

The text of this book was composed in Nobel and Avenir

Printed in China

10 9 8 7 6

HNA
harry n. abrams, inc.
a subsidiary of La Martinière Groupe
115 West 18th Street
New Yok, NY 10011
www.hnabooks.com

To my customers,

who have made Purl more

special to me than

I ever thought possible.

CONTENTS

When an editor from Stewart, Tabori & Chang called me one day at Purl, my knitting shop in New York City, and asked if I wanted to write a book, I was surprised and delighted. While I had often dreamed about authoring a book, I'm sure I wouldn't have started one just then if I hadn't been nudged along by this offer. The editor's idea was a book of knitted gifts that could be completed in about ten hours or less. Although I agreed to work on a proposal, I have to admit that at first I was suspicious of the concept. I worried that quick projects would limit my creativity, that they weren't quite "real." I'd always felt that knitting should be about the process, not about cranking out finished pieces in a short time.

But as it turned out, this book has been a revelation for me. Creating these simple patterns that knit quickly but are also special gifts has been inspiring, challenging, and fun. And I know now that if my theme hadn't been quick projects, I never would have finished them by my deadline. As it was, I was still putting the finishing touches on some of them in the wee hours of the morning just before the start of photography.

Just like knitting for a photo shoot, knitting gifts often begins with beautiful visions and ends in a mad dash. Perhaps supplies were purchased months in advance with very good intentions, and yet somehow time has escaped too quickly and the gift must be finished over a weekend, or even in one evening. To minimize the madness, the projects in this book are broken up into chapters based upon how long they take to knit: Less than Two Hours, Two to Four Hours, Four to Six Hours, Six to Eight Hours, and More than Eight Hours. There's also a chapter showing mostly quick but unique and distinctive ways to wrap handknitted gifts. The wrapping is usually the first thing a gift recipient sees so I think it should be special—but definitely not hard or time-consuming to create.

All of the projects in this book were tested and timed by experienced knitters. And, oftentimes, they were—true to this book's theme—knitted at the last minute, thus as quickly as possible. If you are a beginning knitter or not wanting to knit at a particularly fast pace, then you might want to leave yourself more time as insurance. Some patterns include a range of sizing; in most cases, the sample was knitted in the smallest size. Remember, the larger the size, the more time it will take to knit. If you are looking for the quickest projects possible, go straight to the Less-Than-Two-Hour chapter.

While the core of this book is, of course, the projects, the other chapters are also important to me. They are based on my experiences with my customers at Purl. Often, they come in and are dazzled by the colors of yarn lining nearly every inch of wall space but they are fearful of trying something new. They worry that they are not "good with color" or that the person they are knitting for might not like the color they choose. To me, working with color is one of the great joys in life, and I wrote the Exploring Color chapter in hopes of giving people the inspiration and confidence to experiment with it on their own. Similarly, I find that many of my customers—at least when they're new to the shop—are not confident in their knitting knowledge. For that reason, I wrote Knitting Basics, which is not meant to be a comprehensive reference but rather a compilation of answers to questions that I hear every day at Purl. On the Recommended Reading list on page 138 are several reliable, comprehensive technical reference titles.

There are few more touching ways to show someone you care than to knit something for them by hand. Somehow the stitches we create are able to convey sentiments for which words don't always suffice. I hope the patterns in this book will help you to express yourself to those who are dear to you. At its heart, this is not simply a book of patterns, it is my gift to you. My wish is that it will give you the inspiration and confidence to explore and create unique projects for your loved ones on your own.

Happy Knitting!

EXPLORING COLOR

Customers at Purl are usually mesmerized when they walk into the shop for the first time and see the vibrant colors of yarn that line nearly every inch of wall space. Particularly in urban environments like New York City, the experience of being surrounded by a wide spectrum of rich and subtle color can be remarkable and joyful. And yet I find even customers who love color are often wary of working with it. Many seem to feel overwhelmed when faced with a lot of choices. Some believe there is a right and wrong way to mix and combine colors—and they're not confident in their abilities. When choosing yarn for gifts, they face the added challenge of selecting colors they like to work with and with which the gift recipient will be pleased.

Personally, I believe color is a gift given to all of us by nature and is something we can take great pleasure in sharing with others. Part of the reason I opened Purl—and decided to write this book—was to share my passion for color and to inspire people to explore it in ways that are new to them.

A New Perspective

When selecting color for a project, people often approach their decision-making by looking for colors that "match" or "go together." I often find it more helpful to look at colors from the perspective of how they are different. To heighten my awareness of how colors differ, I think about the concepts of color relativity, complementary color, related color, chroma, and value.

Understanding Color Relativity

Early in our childhoods most of us are taught how to identify the primary colors, which are red, yellow, and blue. If we're lucky, we are also taught that by mixing two of these primary colors together, we'll get the secondary colors, specifically, red + yellow = orange, yellow + blue = green, and blue + red = violet. However, one thing many of us are surprised to discover is that there really isn't such a thing as a "pure" or "true" color. To understand this concept, ask a group of ten knitters to find yarn that is "true primary red" and compare the results. Most likely you'll be looking at ten different shades of red. If you look at these ten reds together you will start seeing how they differ from each other. Some will look more violet, some more orange. Some will be quite vibrant, others will appear to be dull. This is because our experience of individual colors changes according to their context. This changing perception of individual colors is called the relativity of color. Relativity can make color seem mysterious, unpredictable, and sometimes intimidating, but it also plays a big role in what ultimately makes working with color so rewarding.

Using the Color Wheel to Understand Complementary and Related Colors

The color wheel is a helpful tool in fostering our understanding of color. On a basic wheel, red, yellow, and blue make up the primary colors from which every other color is made. The secondary colors are made of mixtures of the primaries, as explained earlier. Starting with yellow at 12 o'clock, blue at 4 o'clock, and red at 8 o'clock, the secondary colors would fall like this: green would be at 2 o'clock, violet at 6 o'clock, and orange at 10 o'clock.

I have put together a color wheel of yarn samples that follows this arrangement (see right), but you can see that in many places the samples don't necessarily flow perfectly from one color to the next. This is because in practice both pigments (the minerals and plants that actually constitute dyes) and fibers have irregularities and impurities in them that give us colors that are more complex than simple red, orange, yellow, green, blue, and violet, and these complex colors are often more beautiful as well. Notice that the yellows are directly across from the violets. Yellow and violet are complementary colors. The same goes for blue and orange as well as red and green. The colors between the primary and secondary colors (known as the tertiary colors) are also directly across from their complements. Colors that are opposite each other on the color wheel are described as complementary colors because the visual relationship between them is very dynamic.

Left: Child's Rainbow Scarf (page 56)
Below: Purl Scarf (page 80)
Right: Super-Easy Leg Warmers (page 54)

Oftentimes complementary colors can seem to vibrate when placed next to one another. If you look at paintings by Claude Monet you will find that he often used combinations of complementary colors in his work, which is one of the reasons why his paintings are so striking. The Child's Rainbow Scarf (see above) is a good example of knitting with complementary colors to create a very dynamic relationship. Part of what makes this scarf fun is that the colors of the yarn are bright and hot, but what really makes this project zing is that these vibrant colors are just about true complements of one another, so that each stripe visually vibrates against the next.

Working with colors that neighbor each other on the color wheel can produce more subtle results. Between yellow and orange you can find an infinite number of colors from yellow-orange to orange-yellow. These are related colors, or colors of the same family. Working with many colors of the same family in one project is a great way to add depth to the overall color of your project; your mind's eye seeks out the difference between the colors and mixes them together, creating a visually rich experience. This way of

working with color is what inspired me to create the Purl Scarf. In the Venetian red version of this scarf (see below), the base color is a pink tone, and it is blended together with a vibrant orange laceweight mohair, as well as a brick red worsted-weight mohair. Together, the effect of these three colors is both rich and quiet. In the celadon version of the Purl Scarf (see page 80), the colors are more closely related, and the effect is more subtle. Adding a strand or two of laceweight mohair not only makes this project softer in texture, it also adds softness to colors that are flat or monochromatic (monochromatic means one-colored, and fibers that are monochromatic are those that are not heathered, and those whose color does not vary as hand-dyed yarns do). The Super-Easy Leg Warmers (see right) also benefit from this technique. The base yarn is a monochromatic medium blue, but it is knit with a strand of very fine mohair in a slightly richer blue. The ribbing in this pattern adds its own depth to the overall color of the piece,

but with the mohair knit in, the color takes on a very special quality. The final color almost seems to glow as the lighter color shines through the slightly richer mohair. If I had added a strand of laceweight mohair in a much darker blue or in a complementary color, the result would not have been as luminous, but would have, instead, looked more like an allover heathered color (which of course is an effect with its own beauty).

Practically speaking, when looking at colors to blend together, it is helpful to twist the separate strands together rather than just holding two skeins next to each other. You'll often be surprised by the results. Usually I find that customers end up selecting more vibrant colors when they explore the relationship between the colors by twisting strands together.

Understanding Chroma

Another color concept at work in the Venetian red version of the Purl Scarf is the contrast of chroma. To understand chroma, think of a ripe Meyer lemon, then think of freshly squeezed lemonade. The bright and vivid yellow of the lemon is much more vibrant than the lemonade. The difference between these colors is their chroma. The lemon is high in chroma; the lemonade is low in chroma. Conceptually, a highly chromatic color is one that hasn't been mixed together with its complement. In the Venetian red Purl Scarf, the brick red mohair is much lower in chroma than the bright orange laceweight mohair, or even the slightly earthy pink of the handspun wool. The more vibrant colors of the pink yarn and orange laceweight yarn are luminous underneath the less chromatic brick red mohair. A color that is low in chroma is one that is made when its opposite color is mixed in, which slightly "grays" or breaks the color.

All grays are made up of primary colors combined with relatively equal amounts of their complements. For example, gray can be made up of red mixed with green. The same is true of blue mixed with orange and yellow mixed with violet. When we think of gray we often imagine a flat lifeless battleship color, when in reality gray, being made up of complementary colors, can be one of the most rich and beautiful colors of all. Imagine a naturally warm brown fiber dyed in a bath of vivid green. This will result in a kind of gray that one would hardly call dull and lifeless!

Browns, similar to grays, are made up of mixtures of the primary colors. Unlike gray, which is a mixture of two complementary colors in relatively equal amounts, brown is made up of all three primary colors in similar amounts, usually with one slightly dominating the others. Compare dark chocolate with milk chocolate, for instance. Dark chocolate is more blue; milk chocolate is more red. Because it is really a mixture of all three primaries, brown, like gray, exists in an enormous spectrum of rich variations.

There is no such thing as a "true" or "pure" color. At right we have five different reds and three different greens. The Ombre Alpaca Blanket at left (and on page 118) is a study in browns.

Understanding Color Value

All colors can be light or dark, which is known as the value of the color. Whites and most yellows are inherently light in value though some are darker than others; blacks and deep blues are typically the darkest in value. Most basically, color value is changed by adding white to a color (or using less pigment in the case of dyeing), which lightens it. All colors can appear in an infinite range of values. I created the Ombre Alpaca Blanket (see above) to explore the relationship among browns in different values. This project creates a rich spectrum of browns, in which your mind's eye begins to seek out the different color relationships among the browns. You might notice that the darkest brown begins to look slightly bluish, the medium looks a bit more red, the camel color seems to be quite yellow. When I was working on this blanket I kept thinking of it as a "brown rainbow."

Your Turn

Color is full of surprises. If you're in a hurry when you are picking out yarn for a project, playing around with color might not be an option and you might want to stick to the colors suggested in the pattern without trying anything else. But if you have some time to explore, I encourage you to try playing with color, applying the theories and ideas I've described here. But don't let any of this convince you that there is a right and wrong way to put colors together. Think of your understanding of the relativity of color, complementary color, chroma, and value as a set of tools that helps you make color choices.

When shopping for yarn, or when going through your stash for a project, explore a variety of color ideas by pulling several different skeins out, placing them next to one another, moving colors around, and substituting different colors to produce new relationships. Notice the relationships between and among the colors whether you like them together or not. When you find something that pleases you, try twisting different strands together to see the effect. You might discover that you have an affinity for playing with chroma, or perhaps you prefer to mix complementary colors together more than you like staying with a single color family. Whatever the case, the main point of the exploration is for you to find what works for you. The more you work with color in your knitting the more you will find your own unique method for applying it in your projects. Ultimately, the more you develop your own idiosyncratic understanding of color, the more joyous your knitting experience will be.

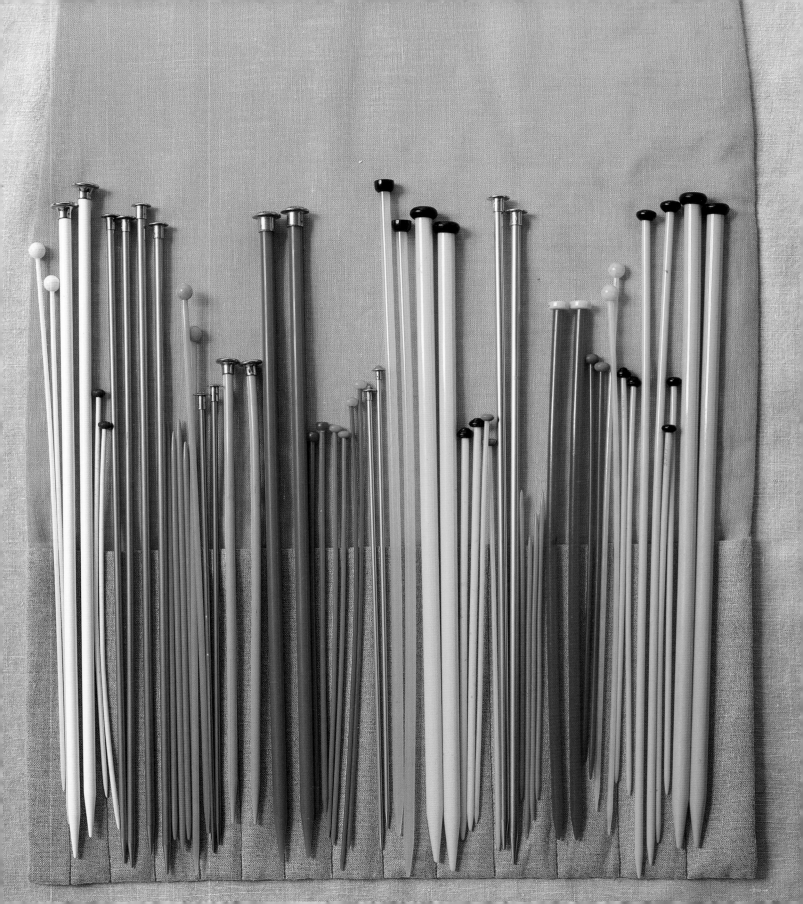

KNITTING BASICS

As a yarn shop owner, I spend a lot of time answering the same questions posed by different customers. In this chapter, I have tried to address many of these questions clearly and simply. For more in-depth discussions of these topics, refer to your favorite reference books or the books I recommend on page 138.

NATURAL FIBERS

Even the most quickly created simple project can become a treasured gift if made with beautiful yarn. I love natural fibers and that is mainly what I knit with and sell at Purl. Although the occasional synthetic fiber has its place and use, I am much more drawn to the unique beauty of the fibers given to us by nature. Many people worry that natural fibers are difficult to clean and maintain, but by following a few simple guidelines (see page 22) natural fibers generally age beautifully. Following is an overview of each of the fibers used for the projects in this book.

Wool

Many people immediately think of wool when they think of knitting; in fact, some people mistakenly call all types of yarn "wool." Wool is shorn from sheep, each of the hundreds of sheep breeds growing fiber with its own distinct characteristics. In fact, you could probably spend a lifetime learning about all of the different types of wool. Merino is generally considered the most luxurious wool because it tends to be especially fine, soft, and smooth. Wool is highly durable, warm, and insulating and is able to hold its warmth even when saturated with water. Because of its natural elasticity, I think wool is the perfect fiber for beginners.

Alpaca

The alpaca is a smaller relative of the camel and the llama. I love alpaca yarn because it is very soft, warm, and smooth, and feels so lovely slipping through my fingers while I am knitting. Alpaca has a plush quality; it is more fuzzy than wool, but less fuzzy than angora or mohair. Because of its warmth, luxurious hand, and relatively inexpensive price, some people call it "poor man's cashmere." Alpaca comes in twenty-two natural colors, ranging from off-white to rich black, and when dyed the colors are especially rich. Knit at

the correct gauge, alpaca drapes elegantly, which gives pieces made with it an added feeling of luxury. Because alpaca fiber is very dense and can be very heavy, it is often blended with other lighter fibers. Alpaca is not necessarily a great yarn for beginners, as it is slightly slippery, requiring a little practice to achieve even stitches. It is also easy to tighten alpaca stitches too much if you tend to pull firmly on your yarn as you work. If you are a tight knitter, try knitting alpaca on a needle slightly larger than the size recommended for your project.

Cashmere

This deluxe fiber comes from a particular type of goat, but there is no such thing as a pure cashmere breed. Most goats, with the exception of angoras (who produce mohair), have a dual coat that consists of outer guard hairs and a downy undercoat. The fine fibers of this undercoat must meet strict industry standards to qualify as cashmere. Good-quality cashmere is seductively soft, silky, warm, and lightweight, and drapes beautifully. It is generally a dream to work with (although some of the finer kinds can be a bit slippery and delicate), but it can be very expensive. Fortunately, there are a variety of cashmere blends that have many of

cashmere's endearing qualities but are more affordable. A good way to evaluate the softness of a cashmere yarn (or any other yarn being considered for knitting) is to hold it up to a sensitive area of your body, such as your cheek or neck.

Mohair

Mohair, a wonderfully fluffy, lustrous fiber, comes from the Angora goat. Kid mohair, which comes from the first and second shearings of the goat, is generally softer and finer than adult mohair, which can be a bit coarse. Fluffy mohair looks dramatic knitted on its own, and because it has a lustrous sheen and takes dye well, it is also blended with other fibers to give matte colors more depth and texture. The fuzziness of mohair obscures mistakes (at times, it can even keep a dropped stitch from unraveling), but it can also be challenging for beginners because it is difficult to see individual stitches. I have found that beginners have better luck when they combine mohair with a yarn made out of another less-fluffy fiber, such as wool, or when they knit it on larger needles than the label recommends.

Angora

Silky, soft, lightweight, very fluffy, and very warm, angora is the fur of the Angora rabbit. Because its fluffiness can obscure stitches and because it is very slippery, angora can be challenging for beginners. On the other hand, the fluff of angora can also hide mistakes. It is great to use for details around garment edges, such as at the wrist or collar, or for small projects like baby booties. Pure angora typi-

cally comes in a rich array of jewel tones. Angora is usually sold in small quantities because it is expensive to harvest and spin. Often, to get the effect of angora without spending a lot of money, I'll choose an angora blend. One of my favorites is Classic Elite's 50% angora, 50% wool blend called Lush.

Silk

Most commercial silk comes from a domesticated silkworm (actually the caterpillar stage of the silk moth) called the *Bombyx Mori*. Because of its intense luster and smoothness, silk looks almost jewel-like when dyed. It drapes beautifully, but its lack of elasticity can make it a challenging fiber for beginners. I reserve silk for special projects that call for a bit of glamour and shine. Be sure not to knit silk too tightly as the result can be unpleasantly stiff.

Cotton

Cotton is a plant fiber that I like for summer knitting and for projects that get washed a lot. Cotton can be more difficult to work with than wool and other animal fibers because it has almost no elasticity. It can also be unforgiving, showing every mistake, although many imperfections can be dealt with by proper blocking when the piece is completed. Cotton knitting yarn usually comes in relatively fine gauges because cotton fiber is dense and heavy compared to animal fiber. However, new, lofty cottons that can be knit at bigger gauges have started to appear on the market recently. There are also some very beautiful organic, undyed cottons in earth tones of ecru, green, and camel.

Linen

Linen fiber comes from flax, a long grasslike plant, and is one of the strongest fibers around. The length and strength of the fiber are two reasons why linen ages so beautifully. It doesn't fray or develop a fuzzy nap (as some cottons do) even after repeated washings, drapes beautifully, and absorbs moisture. Linen absorbs moisture more readily than cotton, which means it can keep humidity and heat away from the skin. Like cotton, it can be challenging to work with because it is inelastic. My favorite linen is Euroflax from Louet Sales. It comes in a couple of different weights and a huge spectrum of gorgeous colors, and is easy to care for. Linen can even be washed and dried by machine; in fact, the more times it is washed, the softer and more beautiful it becomes.

CARING FOR NATURAL FIBERS

At least once a day a customer at Purl picks up a yarn from the shelf and asks, "Is this washable?" The answer is that all natural fibers are washable as long as they are washed properly. Wool can get wet without shrinking—ask any sheep that has been out in the rain!

When washing any fiber, use a very gentle soap such as baby shampoo, dish soap (not antibacterial), soap flakes such as Ivory Snow, or a rinse-free detergent formulated especially for handknits; I like to use Wool Mix from Australia. I find Woolite unsatisfactory for handknits made from natural fibers. Similarly, I do not recommend dry cleaning because it is a harsh process that can compromise the hand of natural materials and make once-soft fibers feel rough and itchy.

Before washing, record the measurements of your piece so that you can block it correctly once it is ready to dry. Run cool water in either a large basin or in the tub of a washing machine—enough water so that you will be able to submerge the handknit completely. Add the soap or detergent and allow to dissolve. Add your handknit (in a mesh bag if you are putting it in a washing machine) and soak for about five minutes, with very little or no agitation. You can gently knead the fabric in the water with your hands to loosen dirt and oils, but avoid vigorous agitation (one of the primary causes of felting and shrinking).

If you are washing with a rinse-free detergent, at this point you can simply run the spin cycle on the machine to drain out the water. If you are washing with a soap that needs to be rinsed out, drain all water from the basin, then gently press down on the handknit (do not wring or twist it) to remove excess water. Remove your handknit from the basin, supporting it with your hands to avoid stretching the fab-

ric. Refill the basin with water, then put the handknit back in and press on it to remove more soap; repeat with fresh water until the water runs clear. Always remove the handknit from the basin before adding water because water running rapidly over fibers can felt them. When the piece has been sufficiently rinsed, either run the handknit (in a mesh bag) through the washing machine spin cycle, or roll it in a series of dry towels, changing the towels as they become saturated.

To dry handknits made from animal fibers (such as wool, mohair, alpaca, etc.), place on a flat surface away from sunlight or heat. Shape to match the measurements you took before washing. Allow your work to dry thoroughly. If desired, use rust-proof pins to pin the wet handknit to the desired shape on a towel or blocking board (a flat board made out of a porous material, usually printed with a grid measured in 1-inch increments).

Handknits made from plant fibers (such as cotton or linen) can be laid out to dry as above, or they can be thrown in the dryer, which often softens them nicely. Turn them inside out to preserve the appearance of the right side of the fabric, and make sure to remove the items from the dryer while they are still slightly damp, then lay flat to finish drying. This will prolong the life of the piece, especially if it is cotton, which can develop a fuzzy nap (a sign of the fibers breaking down) if left in the dryer too long.

SUBSTITUTING YARNS

In this book I've suggested yarns for each pattern, however you may want to make substitutions. If you want your project to look as similar as possible to the one in the photo, then be sure to pick a yarn that works up at the same gauge and is very similar in character to the suggested yarn. Look for the same or similar fiber content, yarn structure, and yards per same skein weight. If the substitute yarn is markedly different, the gauge, drape, and/or texture of the project are likely to be affected. Of course, this doesn't mean that it is wrong to substitute yarns; sometimes experimentation is an exciting way to learn about the unique properties of different yarns. But, it is yet another reason to always swatch before you begin a project. That way, you'll have a good sense of how the yarn looks, feels, and behaves, and you'll know whether it works up into a pleasing fabric at the specified gauge.

Because of different characteristics, as mentioned above, yarns that knit to the same gauge may not necessarily have the same number of yards in the same weight skein. For this reason, you should buy the same amount in yards or meters of the substitute yarn, not the same number of skeins.

To find the total amount of yarn needed, multiply the yardage in the original yarn by the number of skeins specified. Divide the total by the yardage of the substitute yarn, and round the result up to the next whole number to determine how many skeins you need of the replacement yarn. For example, you are considering a project that calls for ten 50-gram skeins of wool yarn with 110 yards (100 meters) per skein. You would like to substitute a cotton yarn that knits to the correct gauge, but has 90 yards (82 meters) in 50 grams. Multiply the original wool yarn's yardage by the ten skeins required, and you will see that you need a total of 1100 yards (1000 meters). If you divide the total yards needed by the yardage of the cotton yarn, the result is about 12.2 skeins, so you should purchase 13 skeins. If you simply bought the same number of skeins of the cotton substitute, or ten 50-gram skeins, you would only have 900 yards (820 meters), which is significantly less than required.

Sometimes you may end up with more yarn than necessary, but it is always better to have leftovers than to run short. Usually running out of yarn one time is all it takes to encourage most of us to buy extra, but even experiencing this dilemma once is too many times! Many yarn shops will allow you to return unused balls in their original condition for store credit for up to six months; always be sure to check the shop's return policy before purchasing your yarn.

TOOLS

Truthfully, you can get by with very few tools when you knit—only yarn and needles are absolutely crucial. However, it's often easier and more fun to knit when you have just the right gadget to get a particular job done. Here are the tools I think are truly helpful and worth having around.

Needles

Knitting needles are distinguished by type, material, diameter or size, and length. Beginning knitters often ask which kind of needle is best. Ultimately there is no right answer to this question. While some needles might work better than others for specific fibers, each knitter will develop his or her own preferences over time.

Needle Types

Straight needles have a point on one end and a stopper at the other end to keep stitches from falling off; they are typically used for knitting flat pieces back and forth. Double-pointed needles have a point on each end, and are generally shorter than straight needles. Double-pointed needles usually come in sets of four or five needles, and are used to knit small items in the round like socks, sleeve cuffs, and hats. Circular needles look like two short needles connected by a cable, and they can be used to knit larger items in the round (like a sweater body), or to knit back and forth on more stitches than might fit comfortably on ordinary straight needles (as for an afghan or throw). You may also come across jumper needles, which are less common. They resemble a hybrid between straight and circular needles, with a short needle section at one end of a short length of cable like a circular needle, but with a stopper at the other end like a straight needle. They are used for working back and forth in rows like straight needles, but can accommodate more stitches on the cable section than will fit on the shank of a straight needle.

Many of the patterns in this book are knitted in the round on circular needles. I find that circular needles save me an enormous amount of time and give my knitting a nice, re-fined look because I don't have to sew many pieces of a project together. I personally love Skacel's Addi Turbo circular needles and I use them for everything, even back-and-forth knitting. I find the short length of the needle section to be especially easy to manipulate, and I like the way the knitting sits in my lap, saving a bit of strain on my wrists. They are also great for travel because your knitting doesn't fall off the needle as easily, and they don't poke your neighbor.

Needle Materials

Many beginners seem to enjoy using short bamboo needles because they are the least slippery of the different types of needles, and their shortness makes them relatively easy to control. Bamboo needles are also warm to the touch and are made of a natural material, which many people find desirable. Wooden needles are available in birch, and exotic hardwoods such as rosewood or ebony, and are also nice, although they can be a bit more slippery than bamboo. Flexible plastic or other man-made materials are great for those with joint problems because they are lightweight, warm up quickly to the touch, and conform slightly to the hands. Metal needles usually have the most slippery surface of all, which is great if you want to knit quickly. I recommend that you try as many different types of needles as you can to discover which ones work best for you.

Needle Diameter or Size

Knitting needle sizes are determined by the diameter of the needles along the main part of the shaft. Sizes are often given in more than one system. American and Canadian/British needles employ two different numbering systems, while European and needles from other parts of the world use the actual metric measurement of the needle to indicate size. The patterns in this book give both the American needle size and the metric equivalent.

Needle Length

Shorter lengths of straight needles are good for small projects like narrow scarves; long needles are required for sweaters and other wide projects that may have a lot of stitches. Double-pointed needles come in different lengths from 3" (7.5 cm) for glove tips up to 10" or 12" (25 or 30 cm) that can even accommodate small sweaters. The most commonly available and versatile length for double-pointed needles is about 7" or 8" (18 or 20 cm). Whether you use a set of four or five needles is usually a matter of personal preference, but if a pattern requires that the stitches be arranged a certain way on a specific number of needles, the materials list should tell you whether the project requires a set of four or five. Circular needles are available from 8" to 60" (20 to 150 cm) long to accommodate a wide range of projects knit in the round. The length of the circular needles you choose should be slightly less than the measurement around your project so the stitches will bunch together comfortably and slide easily around the needle; if the stitches are too stretched out they will be tight and difficult to move on the needle.

Measuring Tape

Every knitter should have a good measuring tape with inches printed on one side and centimeters printed on the other. I like measuring tapes where the first mark starts a bit in from the end of the tape so that an accurate reading from the very first inch is possible. Measuring tapes made out of plastic or fiberglass tend to hold their shape longer and give more consistent measurements than fabric tapes, which can stretch over time.

Needle Gauge

After my measuring tape, my needle gauge is the tool I use most. A needle gauge measures the diameter of knitting needles so that you can determine their size, which is useful when the size has rubbed off or was never printed on the

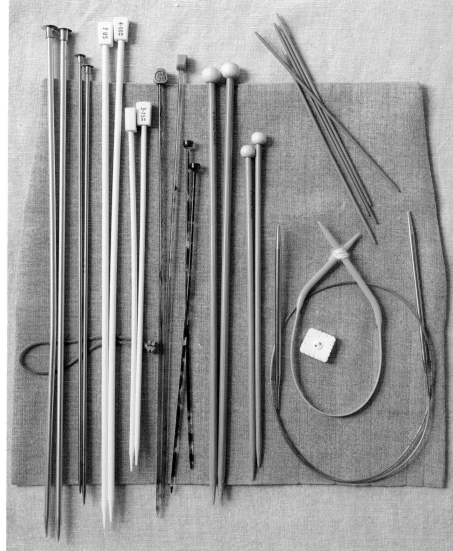

needles in the first place (often the case with metal circular needles). The best gauges have both the US and metric sizes printed on them, and you can find them in both plastic and metal. To use a needle gauge, try the needle in different holes until you find the smallest hole that the needle can pass through easily without any resistance; the size indicated for that hole is the size of your needle.

Crochet Hooks

I keep a full set of crochet hooks in my accessories bag at all times. I use them to pick up dropped stitches and to pick up stitches along the edge of my knitting, such as when applying the neckband to the body of a sweater. I really like hooks with handles that don't get wider at the end so that I can pick up stitches with the hook end, and knit straight off the other end without stretching the stitches. Skacel makes an item called a "cro-hook." This is a tool that looks like a circular needle. It has a crochet hook on one end and a knitting needle on the other. It's the perfect tool for picking up and holding a lot of stitches at once, and you can knit directly off the convenient knitting needle point at the other end when you're finished picking up stitches.

Cable Needle

Cable needles are used to put stitches on hold while you knit other stitches. They come in a variety of different shapes including miniature double-pointed needles, small double-points with recesses or grooves in the center, or the letters U or J. An example of a J-shape cable needle is shown in the photograph at right. You can also use a regular double-pointed needle of any type, as long as it's a few sizes smaller than the needle you are using for the main knitting to prevent the stitches from stretching. Most knitters develop a personal preference for a certain kind of cable needle.

Point Protectors

These "caps" for knitting needles keep stitches from falling off the needles when you are not working on them and also help to keep the tips of bamboo and wooden needles from becoming rough or dull. They can have a strictly utilitarian bullet shape, or look like little teddy bears, tiny sweaters, or miniature socks. For double-pointed needles there are point protectors that come with two caps held together by a stretchy band in order to slip over both ends. The main feature to look for in a point protector is that it is snug enough to fit securely on your needle points without falling off and allowing stitches to escape.

Bobbins

A yarn bobbin can be anything on which you wind a few yards of yarn for working a separate section of color into your knitting. Bobbins are sold in numerous shapes, including bigger versions of sewing machine spools, little dog bones, or fish. You can even use a length of drinking straw for a yarn bobbin, with a slit cut in one end to secure the yarn tail. Bobbins are very useful when working vertical color changes or when using small amounts of different colors across a row in an intarsia design. Usually, the bobbins hang on the wrong side of the work by short lengths to avoid tangling. As you need each bobbin, you release enough yarn to work the stitches required, and then secure the yarn again so the bobbin doesn't unwind. For pieces that use many different colors, bobbins can be much easier to use than large balls of yarn.

Stitch Markers

There are many kinds of stitch markers, only two of which are shown here. The first kind is a ring marker: it goes around your needle between stitches and when you come to it you know that you have something to do, usually an increase or decrease. When you reach your ring marker you simply slip it from the left-hand needle to the right-hand needle, and then do the technique indicated. The other kind of stitch marker shown here is a split ring marker. These can be used the same way as regular ring markers, but they can also be inserted into your work anyplace, anytime, often to mark individual stitches, remind you of the placement of something later, or to keep track of the front and back of your work.

Row Counter

A row counter is a tool that keeps count of the rows worked, but only if you remember to advance it at the completion of every row. They come in barrel shapes that fit on the end of a needle, "clicker" types that you squeeze to click off your progress each row, or cribbage board affairs that can keep track of several different things at once, like a series of increases or decreases, in addition to just rows.

Stitch Holders

Stitch holders are used to put live stitches on hold so that you can come back to them later. If you don't have any stitch holders, you can always slip your live stitches onto a piece of scrap yarn, although sometimes getting them back on the needle can be fiddly. I often use a small size circular needle for this, with a rubber band to hold the two ends together.

This way, I can knit right off the end of the circular needle when I'm ready to retrieve the held stitches. It's a good idea to have some stitch holders in a few different lengths to accommodate different purposes, like small holders for thumbholes in mittens, and longer holders for the stitches placed on hold for neck shaping.

Sharp Embroidery Scissors

A pair of good sharp embroidery scissors is always useful for cutting a piece of yarn, especially cotton, linen, and silk (which most of us can't break with our hands), or trimming yarn ends after they've been woven into the back of the work.

Rust-Proof Blocking Pins

Blocking pins are usually longer than straight pins so they can hold a piece of knitting in place securely, and they have bigger heads so that they are easy to see and remove from the knitting when finished. A garment that has been blocked well is always simpler to sew together than one that hasn't been blocked; blocking pins help to ensure professional-looking results. (For more about blocking, see page 33).

Finishing Needles

(also known as tapestry needles and yarn needles)
Finishing needles look like large sewing needles with big eyes. They are necessary for sewing up your work as well as weaving in your ends. There are a variety of styles; I prefer the metal bent-tip type. The metal slips easily through your knitting, and the bent tip makes it a little easier on your hands and wrists when sewing up a large piece. I find that the easiest way to thread a yarn or tapestry needle is to fold the end of the yarn down and push the folded bit through the eye. This way you will get the entire strand through the eye, and not split the yarn into individual plies.

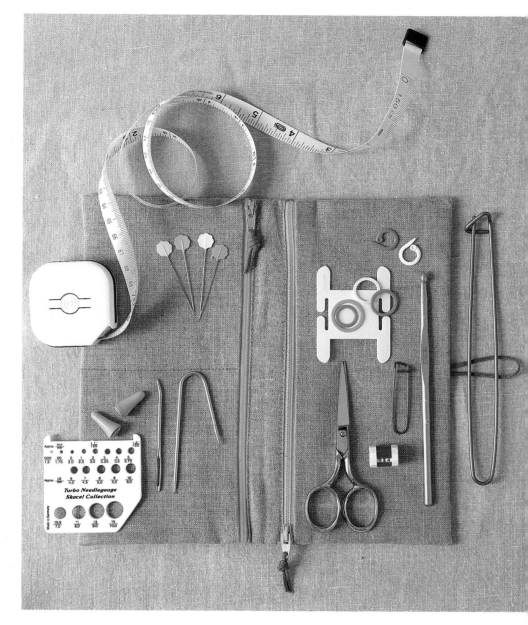

KNITTING FROM A PATTERN

Every day customers tell me that they've been knitting for years and yet they don't know how to read a pattern. Many new knitters feel that knitting from a pattern is simply too advanced for them, which is nearly never true. All anyone needs to know to read a pattern is the meaning of any abbreviations, and how to understand sections where a set of stitches is repeated. Once understood, patterns look less like calculus and more like an exciting way to enrich the knitting experience.

Understanding Abbreviations and Repeats

People often ask me why patterns aren't simply written out in full, clear sentences. Patterns are written in an abbreviated fashion so that they don't end up going on for pages and pages. Also, the more you knit from patterns, the more you will find yourself anticipating what comes next, and the less you will want to be bogged down by reading whole sentences again and again. Marking off sections of the pattern to be repeated is another type of knitting shorthand. Rather than saying "k2, p1, k2, p1, k2, p1, k2, p1, k2, p1," the pattern might instruct you to repeat k2, p1 five times, which is quicker to take in at a glance and is less likely to lead to a mistake.

Different pattern companies and publications have their own sets of abbreviations and ways of punctuating repeats. There is a movement in the knitting industry to standardize the abbreviations used in patterns, but this is a difficult task because everyone has his or her own opinion about which is the clearest way to explain and abbreviate a technique. This book uses the standard abbreviations recently published by the Craft Yarn Council of America. You can find the key to all of the abbreviations in this book on the right. Always take a minute to familiarize yourself with any glossaries or explanations that accompany a pattern before you start. The most basic abbreviations you will find are "k" and "p" for knit and purl. "K2" and "p2", or "k" and "p" followed by another number, mean to knit or purl that number of stitches. Repeats in these patterns can be indicated by an asterisk (*) or are marked off in brackets ([ ]).

Common Abbreviations

BO	bind off
CC	contrast color
CO	cast on
cont	continue
circ	circular needles
dec	decrease
dpn	double-pointed needle
inc	increase
k	knit
k2tog	knit two stitches together (a right-slanting decrease)
k2tog tbl	knit two stitches together through the back loops (a left-slanting decrease)
kf&b	knit into the front and back of the same stitch (an increase)
m	marker
M1	make one stitch by lifting the strand between the two needles by inserting the tip of the left needle from front to back; knit the lifted strand through the back loop (an increase)
MC	main color
p	purl
pm	place marker
psso	pass slipped stitch over
rnd	round
RS	right side of knitted fabric
sl	slip the next st as if to purl from left needle to right needle, without working it
sl1, k1, psso	slip one stitch as if to purl from left needle to right needle, knit the next stitch, pass slipped stitch over knit stitch and off the right hand needle (a left-slanting decrease)
ssk	slip two stitches individually as if to knit to the right needle, transfer the stitches to the left needle in their new orientation, then knit the two stitches together through the back loops (a left-slanting decrease)
st, sts	stitch, stitches
St st	Stockinette stitch; knit on the right side, purl on the wrong side
tbl	through the back loop
tog	together
WS	wrong side of knitted fabric
wyib	with yarn in back
wyif	with yarn in front
yo	yarnover

Understanding Multiple Sizes

Often knitters are befuddled by the presence of more than one set of numbers in a pattern. When you are knitting garments this is very common. When appropriate, the patterns in this book are written out for several different sizes. The smallest size will always appear before the parentheses, and the larger sizes are inside the parentheses, in order from small to large. If you are working on a pattern with several sizes it is sometimes helpful to go through the pattern before you begin and mark your size with a pencil or highlighter so that you follow the correct knitting instructions for your size.

Understanding Fit

The patterns for all of the garments in this book include Finished Measurements, which means the actual dimensions of the completed garment. Garment "ease" is how much bigger around a sweater is than the body that will wear it. The garments in this book are styled for a relatively close fit, with garment ease of about 1" - 2" (2.5 - 5 cm). This is a more modern fit than is found in patterns from about twenty years ago, which may be as much as 4" - 5" (10 - 12.5 cm) larger around than the intended wearer.

These patterns are written to fit an average range of body sizes comfortably, but can, of course, be custom-fitted. If you think a garment is not the right length for your taste, just knit it longer or shorter. If a garment has waist shaping, you might want to add or remove half the amount of the alteration below the waist shaping, and half the amount above, so the relative position of the waist stays the same. If your project does not have waist shaping, you can just add or remove length above the lower edge trim and before the armholes. The same is true of sleeves; try to do any lengthening or shortening before shaping. For a bell sleeve, make any changes after decreasing the belled cuff, but before beginning to increase for the upper arm. A schematic is provided for each sweater in this book so you can determine the best place at which to make your length adjustments. Be aware that sometimes changing the fit can affect the yarn amounts required or the look of the garment.

Understanding Gauge

The other very crucial element to understand when knitting from patterns is gauge (in British English this term is known as "tension"). At Purl I often see customers glazing over when I first talk to them about gauge. The word "gauge" can be

confusing because it seems to refer to so many different things. There is needle gauge, yarn label gauge, pattern gauge, and the actual knitted gauge you might be getting in your swatch, but they're all really elements of the same idea.

Needle gauge refers to the diameter or size of your needle (see Needle Diameter or Size on page 24). Different needle sizes will make different-sized stitches with the same yarn. The larger the needle, the bigger the stitches will be, so there will be fewer stitches per inch; the smaller the needle, the smaller the stitches will be, and there will be more stitches per inch.

When a pattern states the gauge, it is telling you how many stitches and rows there are in a specific length (usually 4" or 10 cm). This is the gauge that the designer or sample knitter got when they made the garment shown. Most patterns give a suggested needle size, and then say something like "or size to obtain the correct gauge." This means you should use whatever size needles it takes to achieve the same number of stitches and rows per unit with your chosen yarn. Otherwise, your project will not turn out to be the same size as the designer intended.

Most yarns list a recommended gauge on the label. The recommended gauge is there to help you figure out if a particular yarn is appropriate for the pattern you are working with. If the recommended yarn gauge on the label is indicated over 4" (10 cm), the yarn will probably work for your pattern if it is within 1 to 3 stitches in 4" (10 cm) of the gauge of your pattern (of course, you will need to try different needle sizes until you get the gauge called for in the pattern). If there is more than 1 to 3 stitches difference, the yarn is probably not a good match for the project, and your work may turn out looking very different from the pattern.

The swatches in this photograph are all the same size. The gauge at which they are knit ranges from 2 to 7 stitches per inch.

Once you find a yarn that looks like a good fit for your project, the next step is to make a knitted gauge swatch. This will tell you whether your chosen yarn will actually work up to the correct pattern gauge, and it will also let you decide whether you like the resulting fabric at that gauge. To make an accurate gauge swatch, knit a sample using the recommended needle size. (I prefer to make swatches that are actually larger than 4" [10 cm] square.) Then, measure the number of stitches and rows over 4" (10 cm) in three different places around the swatch: one near the bottom, one in the middle and one near the top. Average out the results. If you have more stitches per unit than the pattern gauge, try it again using a larger needle. If you have fewer stitches per unit than the pattern gauge, try a smaller needle.

Again, the correct needle size for you is whatever size will give the correct gauge. Many new knitters assume that the needle size requirements in the pattern or on the yarn label are the size they are supposed to be using, but they are really only a starting point because everyone's knitting style is different. If you know that you tend to be a loose knitter (the stitches are very loose on the needle), you might want to approach every swatch by starting with a smaller needle than recommended. Tight knitters (stitches are very tight on the needle) might want to begin with a larger needle than suggested. Don't worry if you have to use needles that are quite different in size from those recommended; what matters is that you achieve the same number of stitches per unit as indicated in the pattern.

Many things in this book do not require fitting, and for these taking a gauge swatch is not as crucial. For garments that have to be a certain size, however, skip gauge swatches at your own risk! Sometimes knitters feel that working a gauge swatch is a waste of time, but it is actually a huge timesaver. If you know in advance that you have the correct gauge, you won't have to rip out your work because it's the wrong size (although you might for other reasons!). It's a good idea to keep your swatch for a reference throughout a project. Many knitters find that their gauge relaxes and grows a bit as they settle comfortably into a project. I usually find that after a few inches I have to go down a needle size to keep my gauge consistent, so I always keep my swatch handy for checking. It is also convenient to carry your swatch around with you when shopping for buttons.

FINISHING, BEFORE YOU START

Finishing can greatly affect the look of your hard work and is important if you want your efforts to look "handmade" rather than "homemade." I often hear people talking about how difficult finishing is, but really it's not hard if you have learned the correct techniques. There are many things you can do during the knitting phase that will simplify finishing. Following are the techniques I find most useful.

Edge Stitches

Edge stitches, also known as selvedge stitches, make your project easier to finish nicely by giving you a defined edge to follow for seaming. All of the patterns in this book that require sewing up have a selvedge stitch written into the pattern. When using patterns from other sources, I always work a selvedge stitch into my knitting, even if it isn't included in the pattern. To make selvedge stitches, I like to knit the first and last stitch of every single row, whether the pattern says to or not. Some people like to slip the first stitch and knit the last stitch of every row, but I find knitting the stitches at each end to be cleaner.

Increases and Decreases

Working your increases and decreases two or three stitches in from the edges can also simplify sewing seams. Increases and decreases made at the edges of a piece can make it difficult to work the seam the same distance from the edge the whole way along. Just like adding your own selvedge stitches, you can move the increases and decreases a few stitches in from the edge on any pattern.

One thing to keep in mind is that when you work shaping away from the edge, it will show as a decorative increase or decrease after sewing the pieces together. To make shaping look really nice I always do my increases like this: At the beginning of rows, I knit the edge stitch, work the second stitch, then work an increase into the third stitch; at the end of rows, I work an increase on the third stitch from the edge, then work the next stitch, and knit the last stitch. For decreasing, at the beginning of the row I knit the edge stitch, work the second stitch, then work an ssk decrease on the third and fourth stitches; at the end of rows, I knit to the last four stitches, knit two stitches together, work one stitch, and then knit the last stitch. This makes my decreases and increases look neat and professional.

Joining a New Ball of Yarn

When adding a new ball of yarn to your knitting, start the new yarn at the edge of the piece, unless otherwise indicated in the pattern. If you're not sure whether you will have enough yarn to finish a row, measure the remaining yarn to see if it is at least four times longer than the width of the piece you are knitting. If not, start the new ball of yarn before launching into the next row.

Weaving in ends

When I weave in yarn tails, I don't weave them into the seam allowances because this can create bulkiness. Instead, I usually run the ends diagonally through the purl bumps on the inside. This doesn't show on the front, and the ends seem to stay put for a long time.

FINISHING, AFTER YOU FINISH

Seams

Many of the patterns in this book are knitted in the round to avoid seams. However, when a pattern requires sewing up, the most appropriate technique will be indicated. If you only learn one way to sew up pieces, I recommend that you learn mattress stitch (see page 134). I find that mattress stitch looks much more professional than almost any other seaming technique. Other finishing techniques used in these patterns are explained clearly in the text. Complicated or more unusual techniques are illustrated in the Special Techniques section (see page 132).

Blocking

There are several reasons to block. If your stitches are uneven or your knitting looks rumpled, blocking can work miracles. You should always block knitted lace because it opens up the delicate stitches to reveal the full beauty of the pattern. Blocking pieces before sewing them together can sometimes make finishing easier. If your project looks even and smooth before blocking, then you can probably skip this step because it won't affect the look of your finished piece very much.

To block my knitting, I usually pin it flat with blocking pins to folded towels or a blocking board, then spray it with water. I allow the pieces to dry fully before removing the pins. (It is important not to pin it too taut or the sides of the knitting will pull in as it dries.) I don't recommend using an iron to block as I find it can flatten stitches and compromise the texture and hand of natural fibers. For a quick fix, you can hold a steam iron several inches above the pinned-out pieces and steam them gently. Do not let the iron touch the surface of the knitting. Steaming can relax and even out the stitches, but in my opinion, steaming doesn't offer results as good as blocking.

The Gusseted Floor Cushions (page 86) are finished with a decorative and utilitarian crocheted slipstitch edge.

LESS-THAN-TWO-HOUR GIFTS

ANGORA BABY BOOTIES

These booties can be made in less than one hour each, and they do not involve any sewing! One of the techniques used to make these booties is known as double knitting, which is a great way to knit in the round with just two needles. Don't be surprised to see that you will be knitting these booties inside out once you get going.

FINISHED SIZE
To fit up to infant's shoe size US 2.

FINISHED MEASUREMENTS
Foot circumference about 5" (12.5 cm) around, foot length 3½" (9 cm), and 2" (5 cm) from bottom of sole to top of ribbed cuff.

YARN
Approximately 30 yards [27 meters] of yarn to give the correct gauge. Shown here and on page 39 in the following:

Bouton d'Or Angora 100% (100% angora; 37 yards [34 meters] / 10 grams): #119 corail (bright coral), 1 skein.

Bouton d'Or Imperial Infeutrable (100% angora, 61 yards [56 meters] / 10 grams): #99810 cascade (aqua), 1 skein.

Belangor French Angora (100% angora; 33 yards [30 meters] / 10 grams): #801 white or #804 (salmon), 1 skein.

NEEDLES
One set of five double-pointed needles size US 5 (3.75 mm). Change needle size if necessary to obtain the correct gauge.

NOTIONS
Yarn needle, scissors, 2 point protectors.

GAUGE
24 sts and 32 rows = 4" (10 cm) in Stockinette stitch.

Note:
All slipped stitches are slipped as if to purl with the yarn in back.

Toe
CO (cast on) 24 sts (stitches). *K1, slip 1; repeat from * to end. Repeat this row until piece measures 2" (5 cm) from beginning, working an even number of rows so both layers of the double knit toe will be equal. To keep the edges looking nice, at the beginning of each row after the CO row, insert needle into first st, take the working yarn under right-hand needle and around to the back of the work, then knit the first st.

Foot
Redistribute the sts to open the toe up into its two individual layers. Holding two empty double-pointed needles parallel to each other in your right hand, one in front of the other, *slip the first st from the left-hand needle onto the back needle, slip the next st on the left-hand needle onto the front needle; repeat from * until all sts have been slipped to the two double-pointed needles in your right hand. Separate the needles slightly to make sure that the toe of the bootie is open and the sts have been divided into their individual layers. You will notice that the knit side of the fabric is on the inside of the toe.

Heel Preparation
Hold the bootie so that the needle with the working yarn is facing you and coming from the first st on the front needle. With an empty needle in your right hand, take the working yarn under the right-hand needle as before and knit across all 12 sts on back needle. Rotate the work so the former front needle is now in back. Knit the first 3 sts on the new back needle, and transfer them to the needle with the 12 sts just worked. You now have 15 sts on the front needle, 9 sts on the back needle, and the working yarn is coming from the first st on the front needle. The purl side of the fabric is still on the outside.

Next row: On the front needle, k1, p14; with an empty needle p2, k1 from the back needle, and transfer them to the needle with the 15 sts just worked. There will be 18 sts on the front needle, 6 sts on the back needle, and the working yarn is coming from the last st on the front needle. Place a point protector on each end of the back needle to keep the needle from slipping out of the 6 sts while you work the heel.

Heel

Work back and forth in Stockinette stitch on 18 sts for 10 rows, beginning with a knit row, and knitting the first and last st of *every* row to form a garter st selvedge for picking up sts later. On the next row, k9, and turn—two heel needles with 9 sts each. Fold the heel needles together with their knit sides touching and the purl side of the fabric on the outside. With the working yarn coming from the first st on the front needle, use the three-needle bind-off method (see page 133) to join the sts on the two heel needles together up the back of the heel—1 st remains from heel sts after finishing three-needle bind off.

Cuff

Turn bootie right side out, with the knit side of the fabric on the outside. You will have 1 live st on the needle at the back of the heel, and 6 sts on hold for the instep. With RS facing, pick up and knit 8 sts along garter st selvedge. With another needle, knit across 6 sts for instep. With a third needle, pick up and knit 8 sts along other garter st selvedge—23 sts: 9 on first needle, 6 on instep needle, 8 on third needle. Replace point protectors on needle with 6 instep sts, if necessary.

Row 1: Working on the first needle (the one with 9 sts), k2tog, p1, [k1, p1] 3 times to end of needle, turn.
Row 2: [K1, p1] 8 times—22 sts: 8 sts each on two needles, 6 sts on instep needle.
Row 3: Turn, repeat Row 2 along 16 sts.
Row 4: Turn, [K1, p1] 8 times, work [k1, p1] 3 times across 6 instep sts. Continue in the round on all 22 sts, and work 4 rounds of k1, p1 rib as established. Bind off all sts loosely in rib pattern.

Finishing

Weave in all ends. Make second bootie the same as the first.

LINEN TASSELS

Tassels make worthy gifts in and of themselves. They are beautiful and useful as pull chains for lamps and as decorations on drawer handles, and can add a spot of color in an otherwise quiet room. Tassels can also be used as Christmas tree ornaments or embellishments on wrapped gifts, and, of course, tassels can be used to embellish hand-knits, such as along the bottom of a poncho or at the ends of a drawstring.

I like to make tassels out of sportweight linen from Louet Sales because this yarn has wonderful drape, comes in incredible colors, and has an appealing natural texture.

Approximately 5" (12.5 cm) long
and ³/₄" (1.9 cm) diameter.

YARN
Louet Sales Euroflax Originals
Sport Weight (100% linen; 270
yards [247 meters] / 100 grams):
#2234 (berry red), 1 skein makes
approximately 10 tassels.

NOTIONS
Yarn needle, card stock, scissors,
crochet hook size E/4 (3.5 mm)
or F/5 (4.00 mm), small amount
of scrap yarn.

The traditional proportions of a tassel call for the top one-third to be the head and neck, and the lower two-thirds to be the skirt, or loose strands. For a tassel with these proportions, cut a 2" or 3" (5- or 7.5-cm) wide strip of card stock to the desired overall length of the tassel. Draw a line across the card stock about one-third of the way from one short end. Cut two notches ½" (1.3 cm) deep in the bottom short end of the card stock, about 1½" (3.8 cm) apart.

Anchor one end of the yarn in one of the notches, and then wrap the yarn firmly around card stock the long way in close parallel lines from top to bottom until you reach the second notch. Anchor the other end in the second notch and cut yarn. Cut two strands each of linen and scrap yarn about 6" - 8" (15 - 20 cm) long. Thread one length of linen on a yarn needle, and slip the needle underneath the wrapped strands on one side of the cardstock, even with the marked line one-third of the way from the end. Tie the ends of the strand snugly into a square knot. Turn the cardboard over and repeat for the other side. With scrap yarn threaded on a yarn needle, slip the yarn underneath the wrapped strands at the top short edge of the card stock, and tie the ends in a tight square knot to secure the head of the tassel. Tie the bottom of the tassel in the same way, using a piece of scrap yarn. I've found that tassels always seem to come out a bit thicker than I expect, so I try not to wrap too many lengths of yarn around the card stock. These are quick projects, so it doesn't take long to experiment with different proportions to find the effect that pleases you best.

Slip tassel off card stock. Use a 1-yard (1-meter) length of linen yarn threaded on a yarn needle to wrap the neck of the tassel. Begin by inserting the threaded needle through from the inside of the neck to the outside, then insert it from the outside, through to the other side to fasten the two halves of the neck together. Next, wind yarn tightly around the neck, covering the pieces used to secure the tassel neck while it was still on the card stock. Wind smoothly, laying each wrap snugly next to the previous wrap for a neat appearance. When the wrapping is the desired height, pass the threaded needle into the center of the tassel bundle, down through the wrapped neck section, and out the bottom.

Cut through the loops at the bottom of the tassel at the scrap yarn. Trim the end of the neck wrapping yarn to the same length. Make a cord for the tassel by working crochet chain stitch to desired length. Slip crocheted chain through center of the head of the tassel, replacing the scrap yarn used to secure the head. Pull the ends of the chain even and tie the ends in a square knot. Use additional lengths of crocheted chain to attach the tassel to the desired object, such as a lamp pull or package.

POMPOMS

Pompoms, though not knitted, are the perfect embellishment for many knitted gifts, and can also be put to creative uses on their own. Pompoms are a great way to take advantage of yarn leftover from other projects, and can be used on packages, as ornaments, on top of hats, at the ends of scarves, or to finish the ends of a tied cord. When strung together, pompoms can become a delicate necklace, or even a garland on a Christmas tree.

FINISHED MEASUREMENTS
The assortment of pompoms shown here measures approximately 1" (2.5 cm) to 4" (10 cm) in diameter.

YARN
I like to mix together all sorts of colors and textures to make pompoms that look and feel interesting.

NOTIONS
Yarn needle, pompon-making tool or stiff card stock, scissors.

If you have a pompom maker, follow the directions that come with it. I like the Clover brand pompom maker, which makes pompoms in four different sizes. If you purchase one, check to make sure it includes the English translation of the Japanese directions.

If you don't have a pompom maker, or want to try making pompoms without one, there are many ways to do it. The following is my favorite.

Cut a strip of stiff card stock. The width of the finished pompom will be double the width of the cardboard strip along one short side. Cut a notch in each short end to secure the yarn. Wrap the yarn around the strip many times—the more wraps, the fuller and fluffier your pompom will be. Cut a length of yarn about 6" (15 cm) longer than the width of your wraps and thread it on a yarn needle. Slip the needle underneath the wrapped strands along one long edge of the card stock, and pull through, leaving about 3" (7.5 cm) hanging out at each side. Tie the ends of the strand snugly into a single knot and hold, or ask a volunteer to place a helpful index finger on the knot for a moment. Cut the wraps along opposite long edge of the card stock. Pull the knot very tight, and finish with a another single knot to make a square knot. Fluff up the pompom and trim the ends.

To make a strand of pompoms, use one end of a long length to tie off the first pompom. Use the same length of yarn to tie the remaining pompoms, leaving the desired distance between them. Be careful not to cut the connecting strand when fluffing and trimming the pompoms.

The pompoms shown here and on page 34 were made with the following yarns:
Blue Sky Alpaca Sportweight Alpaca and Silk; Koigu Premium Merino and Painter's Palette Premium; Jamieson & Smith 2-Ply Jumper-Weight Yarn; Manos del Uruguay Wool; Jaeger Silk 4-Ply; Plassard Flore; Rowan Kidsilk Haze; and Bouton d'Or Imperial.

KERCHIEF SCARF

This scarf is a simple right-angle triangle knit on the bias. It can be worn around the neck or on the head, or it can be used to wrap a small gift. Because it doesn't take much yarn, this project is an excellent way to use luxurious yarns like fine cashmere without breaking the bank. On the other hand, it can easily be adapted to shawl size if you continue to increase at the end of each row until you have reached your desired width. I have one of these scarves in cotton and one in cashmere, so whatever the season, I can put one on and add color and just the right amount of warmth to my day.

FINISHED MEASUREMENTS
9" (23 cm) high from bottom point to top edge, and
20" (51 cm) across top edge.

YARN
GGH Molina (100% cotton; 110 yards [100 meters] / 50 grams): #9 blue/green mix, 1 skein.

NEEDLES
One set straight needles size US 7 (4.5 mm).
Change needle size if necessary to obtain the correct gauge.

NOTIONS
Yarn needle, scissors.

GAUGE
22 sts and 44 rows (22 garter ridges) = 4" (10 cm) in garter stitch.

Cast on 3 sts. Slip the first st as if to knit, knit to last st, kf&b (knit into front and back of same st to increase 1 st). Repeat every row until there are 110 sts. Bind off all sts. Weave in ends.

That's it!

SWEATER AND STOCKING MINIS

These tiny projects can be given as ornaments or used to decorate a greeting card or a homemade mobile. They can also stand in as a mini-sample of a sweater or Christmas stocking that was promised as a gift, but not quite finished! The window display at Purl includes mini sweaters embroidered with letters spelling out our name.

MINI SWEATER

FINISHED MEASUREMENTS
4¾" (12 cm) from cuff to cuff, 2" (5 cm) from bottom edge to top of neck, and 2" (5 cm) wide across chest.

YARN
Jamieson & Smith 2-Ply Jumper Weight Yarn (100% Shetland wool; 125 yards [114 meters] / 25 grams): 1 skein each of four colors A, B, C, and D will make about 16 - 20 mini sweaters. Shown in #1A natural (A), #52 fuchsia (B), #FC8 dark gold heather (C), and #FC38 russet heather (D).

NEEDLES
One set of five double-pointed needles size US 2 (3 mm). Change needle size if necessary to obtain the correct gauge.

NOTIONS
Yarn needle, scissors, stitch marker, one white pipe cleaner per mini sweater for hanger (optional).

GAUGE
28 sts and 36 rows = 4" (10 cm) in Stockinette stitch. Exact gauge is not critical for this project.

Back and Front (make 2)
With A, CO (cast on) 16 sts onto one double-pointed needle. Working back and forth in rows (do not join for working in the round), work in k2, p2 rib for 2 rows. Change to Stockinette stitch, and work 2-row stripes (knit 1 row, purl 1 row) in the following order: B, C, D, A, B—12 rows completed. Cut yarn, leaving the sts on the needle. Weave in ends and set aside.

Sleeves (make 2)
With B, cast on 12 sts onto one double-pointed needle, leaving an 8" (20-cm) or longer tail for sewing up. Working back and forth in rows, work in k2, p2 rib for 2 rows. Change to Stockinette st, and work 2-row stripes (knit 1 row, purl 1 row) in the following order: C, D, A, B—10 rows completed. Cut yarn, leaving sts on the needle. Weave in ends except for the 8" (20.5-cm) starting tail, and set aside.

Yoke
Rnd (Round) 1: (Joining rnd) Attach C to sts of first sleeve needle with RS facing, k12 sleeve sts, k16 sts from the front, k12 sts from other sleeve, k16 sts from the back—56 sts: 12 sts each on 2 needles for sleeves, and 16 sts each on 2 needles for back and front. Join for working in the rnd, and place marker to indicate the beginning of the rnd.
Rnd 2: With C, knit 1 more rnd.
Rnd 3: Change to D. *K1, ssk, knit to last 3 sts on needle, k2tog, k1; repeat from * for remaining 3 needles—8 sts decreased; 48 sts: 10 sts each on 2 needles for sleeves, 14 sts each on 2 needles for back and front.
Rnd 4: With D, knit 1 more rnd.
Rnds 5 and 6: Change to A, and repeat Rnds 3 and 4—40 sts remain after Rnd 5.
Rnds 7 and 8: Change to B, and repeat Rnds 3 and 4—32 sts remain after Rnd 7.
Rnd 9: Change to C and repeat Rnd 3—24 sts.
Rnds 10 and 11: Work in k2, p2 rib.
Bind off all sts with C in rib pattern.

Finishing
Using cast-on tail from sleeve, sew sleeve and side seam from cuff to underarm, then down the side of the sweater to the cast-on edge. Repeat for other sleeve and side seam. Weave in ends. If desired, fold a pipe cleaner into the shape of a small clothes hanger and place inside of sweater.

MINI STOCKING

FINISHED MEASUREMENTS
About 2½" (6.5 cm) around, and 3" (7.5 cm) long.

YARN
Jamieson & Smith 2-Ply Jumper Weight Yarn (100% Shetland wool; 125 yards [114 meters] / 25 grams): 1 skein each of four colors A, B, C, and D will make about 15 mini stockings. Shown in #FC11 bright green heather (A), #FC12 gold-green heather (B), #52 fuchsia (C), and #1A natural (D).

NEEDLES
One set of four double-pointed needles size US 0 (2 mm). Change needle size if necessary to obtain the correct gauge.

NOTIONS
Yarn needle, scissors, stitch marker, crochet hook size B/1 (2.25 mm) for hanging loop (optional).

GAUGE
32 sts and 40 rows = 4" (10 cm) in Stockinette stitch. Exact gauge is not critical for this project.

STITCH GUIDE
Seed Stitch in the Round (even number of sts)
Rnd (Round) 1: *K1, p1; repeat from * to end.
Rnd 2: *P1, k1; repeat from * to end.
Repeat these 2 rnds for pattern.

Cuff
With A, cast on 20 sts. Divide the sts on 3 needles, 2 needles with 7 sts, and one needle with 6 sts. Join for working in the rnd (round) and place marker to indicate the beginning of the rnd.
Work in seed st for 3 rnds, do not cut yarn A.
Rnd 1: Join B, and knit 1 rnd.
Rnds 2 and 3: *K2 sts with A, k2 sts with B; repeat from * to end.
Rnd 4: With B, knit 1 rnd.
Rnds 5 - 14: With A, knit 10 rnds.
Rnds 15 - 18: Repeat Rnds 1 - 4.

Short-Row Heel
Redistribute sts on 3 needles with the first 10 sts on one needle for the heel, and 5 sts each on the other 2 needles for the instep. Work back and forth in rows on 10 heel sts *only* as follows:
Row 1: (RS) Join C. K10, turn.
Row 2: P9, turn.
Row 3: Yo (yarnover), k8, turn.
Row 4: Yo, p7, turn.
Row 5: Yo, k6, turn.
Row 6: Yo, p5, turn.
Row 7: Yo, k4, turn.
Row 8: Yo, purl to first yo, purl this yo together with the next st, turn.
Row 9: Slip the first st as if to purl, knit to first yo, knit yo together with the next st, turn.
Row 10: Slip the first st as if to purl, purl to first yo, purl yo together with the next st, turn.
Repeat Rows 9 and 10 until all yo's have been worked, ending with a RS row—10 sts. Cut C.

Foot
Redistribute the 10 sts on the heel needle onto 2 needles with 5 sts each, then transfer the remaining 10 sts to one needle for the instep. Join A at the back of the heel, between the 2 needles with 5 sts each, and place marker for new beginning of rnd. Knit 9 rnds.

Toe
Change to color C and knit 1 rnd. Decrease Rnd: On first needle, knit to last 3 sts of needle, k2tog, k1; on second needle, k1, ssk, knit to last 3 sts of needle, k2tog, k1; on third needle, k1, ssk, knit to end—4 sts decreased. Knit 1 rnd even. Repeat the last 2 rnds 2 more times—8 sts. Cut yarn leaving a 6" (15-cm) tail.

Finishing
Thread tail on yarn needle, run the tail through the remaining sts, and pull to draw sts together and close toe. Turn stocking inside out and weave in loose ends. Embroider a snowflake on one side with D as shown. If desired, work a crochet chain for a hanging loop at top edge of stocking.

FELTED POTHOLDERS

These potholders make a thoughtful hostess or housewarming gift along with a gourmet food item. If you can, find out the color scheme of the recipient's kitchen so you can pick your yarn accordingly.

FINISHED MEASUREMENTS
About 8" - 8¼" (20 - 20.5 cm) square, after washing and felting.

YARN
Baabajoes Woolpak Yarns NZ 14 Ply (100% wool; 310 yards [283 meters] / 250 grams): #20 birch (light gray), 1 skein.

Manos del Uruguay (100% hand-spun kettle-dyed wool; 137 yards [125 meters] / 100 grams): #69 hibiscus, #20 Parma, #V cinnamon, and #49 henna, 1 skein each.

Depending on your color combinations, these amounts will make 10 – 12 potholders. A single skein of Woolpak NZ 14 ply will make 4 or 5 solid-color potholders, and a single skein of Manos will make about 2 solid-color potholders

NEEDLES
One set straight needles size US 10½ (6.5 mm).
Change needle size if necessary to obtain the correct gauge.

NOTIONS
Yarn needle, scissors, crochet hook size J/10 (6 mm) for edging (optional).

GAUGE
14 sts and 28 rows (14 garter ridges) = 4" (10 cm) in garter stitch before felting. Exact gauge is not critical for this project.

Cast on 44 sts. Work in garter st (knit all sts every row) until piece measures 12½" (31.5 cm), changing colors to create stripes as desired. Bind off all sts loosely as if to knit. If desired, work a row of single crochet all around the outside edge (see page 137).

Felting Instructions

Set washer for hot wash and medium water level. Add a small amount (about 1 tablespoon) of Wool Mix (a wool wash that is excellent for felting and requires no rinsing) or a mild liquid detergent.

If you just want to felt a few potholders without worrying about perfection, simply place them in a zippered pillowcase or a fine mesh bag (to protect the washing machine from the excess fibers that shed during the felting process) and toss them in. When the cycle is over, remove the potholders, pull gently into shape, and air-dry.

If you want to learn a more meticulous way to felt your knitting, follow the instructions for the Felted Yoga Mat Bag on page 92.

TWO-TO-FOUR-HOUR GIFTS

BABY BONNET

This baby bonnet is so beautiful and special that it's hard to believe how simple it is to make. The body of the bonnet is knitted in the shape of an upside down T, or a horizontal rectangle with a square of fabric removed from each of the upper right and left corners. The edges of the inside angles are brought together and seamed. The contrasting I-cord border also functions as ties for the bonnet. The yarn is Rowan's Kid Classic, a soft blend of wool and kid mohair. The slightly heathered, warm color scheme lends an Early American look to this piece.

FINISHED SIZE
To fit head circumference up to 17 ½" (44.5 cm), about 6 - 24 months.

FINISHED MEASUREMENTS
With bonnet lying flat, 6 ½" (16.5 cm) high from lower edge to top of crown, and 6 ½" (16.5 cm) deep from front I-cord trim to back fold.

YARN
Rowan Kid Classic (70% lambswool, 26% kid mohair, 4% nylon; 151 yards [140 meters] / 50 grams): #817 bear (brown) and #842 peach sorbet (pink), 1 skein each.

NEEDLES
One set straight needles size US 8 (5 mm).
One set straight needles size US 10 (6 mm).
Two double-pointed needles size US 9 (5.5 mm) for I-cord edging.
Change needle size if necessary to obtain the correct gauge.

NOTIONS
Yarn needle, scissors, stitch holder.

GAUGE
21 sts and 28 rows = 4" (10 cm) in Stockinette stitch.

The bonnet begins at the front opening. With MC (main color) and size US 10 (6 mm) needles, using the cable cast-on method (see page 132), CO (cast on) 62 sts. Change to size US 8 (5 mm) needles and establish Stockinette st pattern with garter st selvedges as follows:

Row 1: (RS) Knit.
Row 2: (WS) K1, purl to last st, end k1.
Rows 3 - 10: Repeat Rows 1 and 2 four more times.
Row 11: K1, sl (slip) 1 st as if to purl, k1, psso (pass slipped st over), knit to last 3 sts, k2tog, k1—60 sts.
Row 12: K1, purl to last st, end k1.
Rows 13 - 20: Repeat Rows 1 and 2 four more times.
Rows 21 - 30: Repeat Rows 11 - 20 once more—58 sts after completing Row 21.
Rows 31 - 36: Repeat Rows 11 - 16 once more—56 sts after completing Row 31.
Row 37: BO (bind off) 19 sts, knit to end—37 sts.
Row 38: BO 19 sts, purl to last st, end k1—18 sts.
Rows 39 - 60: For the back flap, repeat Rows 1 and 2 eleven times total—piece measures about 8 ½" (21.5 cm) from beginning to top of 18-st back flap. Place sts on a holder.

With yarn threaded on yarn needle, sew the bound-off edge to the back flap selvedge at each side, beginning at the inner corner of the L-notch formed by the bind-off.

Bottom Edging
With MC and RS facing, using size US 8 (5 mm) needles, pick up (see page 135) 80 sts along bottom neck opening of bonnet as follows: pick up and knit 31 sts along selvedge to holder, knit across 18 sts on holder, pick up and knit 31 sts to end. Work in garter stitch for 6 rows (3 garter ridges). BO all sts loosely.

Knit on I-cord Tie
With CC (contrast color) and a single dpn, CO 3 sts. Work I-cord as follows, using 2 double-pointed needles:

All Rows: Slide sts to opposite end of needle, bring working yarn around behind the needle and k3. Do not turn work. Keep the same side facing you at all times, and pull the working yarn firmly around behind the sts on the needle to form a knitted tube. Work in this manner until I-cord measures 8" (20.5 cm). Work joined I-cord along the front opening edge of bonnet as follows:

All Rows: Slide the sts to opposite end of needle, and bring working yarn around behind the needle as before. K2, sl the 3rd st to right-hand needle as if to purl with yarn in back. With RS of bonnet facing, use the tip of the left-hand needle to pick up 1 loop from the front edge of hat along the original cast-on edge. Knit the picked-up loop from the left-hand needle, then pass the slipped st over—3 sts on right-hand needle.

Repeat this row for every st around the front opening edge of the bonnet, then work plain, unjoined I-cord for 8" (20.5 cm) for other tie. Bind off all sts.

Finishing
Weave in ends.

SUPER-EASY LEG WARMERS

These leg warmers are cozy and soft and look great under a skirt. Part of the reason I am so happy with them is the yarn combination: a basic worsted-weight merino, Cascade 220, that comes in a huge variety of colors, and a laceweight kid mohair-silk blend, Madil Kid Seta, that keeps the leg warmers from feeling itchy and gives the color more depth.

FINISHED SIZE
One size fits all, will stretch to fit up to 15" (38 cm) around.

FINISHED MEASUREMENTS
Circumference about 8" (20.5 cm) around (unstretched), and 26" (66 cm) long.

YARN
Cascade Yarns Cascade 220 (100% wool; 220 yards [201 meters] / 100 grams): #9326 light blue, 2 skeins.

Madil Kid Seta (70% kid mohair, 30% silk; 230 yards [210 meters] / 25 grams): #425 blue bell, 2 skeins.

NEEDLES
One 12" (30-cm) circular needle size US 8 (5 mm).
Change needle size if necessary to obtain the correct gauge.

NOTIONS
Yarn needle, scissors, stitch marker.

GAUGE
23 sts and 24 rows = 4" (10 cm) in k1, p1 rib in the round, with rib relaxed.

With both yarns held together, cast on 46 sts. Join for working in the round, being careful not to twist.

All Rounds: *K1, p1; repeat from * to end.
Work in k1, p1 rib until piece measures 26" (66 cm) long.
Bind off all sts loosely in rib pattern.
Weave in ends.

Work second leg warmer the same as the first.

CHILD'S RAINBOW SCARF

Amazingly, this striped scarf is made with just two skeins of yarn by working two rows from each skein alternately. The multicolored yarn is dyed using a special technique so when knitted it naturally forms an ombre pattern that gradually transitions from one color to the next. Knitting this scarf is especially fun and interesting because you never know which colors of the two skeins are going to end up next to each other.

I worked this scarf in a mistake rib pattern because I like the dynamic relationship between the horizontal stripes of color and the deep vertical ribs, and because it looks the same on both sides. I particularly love the name of this stitch pattern because it demonstrates how sometimes mistakes can be more interesting than perfection.

FINISHED MEASUREMENTS
4" (10 cm) wide (unstretched), and 54" (137 cm) long.

YARN
Noro Kureyon (100% wool; 110 yards [100 meters] / 50 grams): #95 lime/olive/ pink/orange (A), and #130 pink/red/orange/purple (B), 1 skein each.

NEEDLES
One set straight needles size US 9 (5.5 mm).
Change needle size if necessary to obtain the correct gauge.

NOTIONS
Yarn needle, scissors.

GAUGE
16 sts and 23 rows = 4" (10 cm) in Stockinette stitch.
23 sts and 23 rows = 4" (10 cm) in mistake rib pattern.

Stitch Guide
Mistake Rib (multiple of 4 sts, plus 3)
All Rows: *K2, p2; repeat from * to last 3 sts, end k2, p1.

Rows 1 – 2: With color A, cast on 23 sts, and work in mistake rib pattern. (When switching between the two colors, pick up the new color in front of the old color every time. This way the yarns will be carried neatly along the edge of the scarf as you knit.) Do not cut yarn.
Rows 3 – 4: Change to color B and work in mistake rib pattern.
Repeat the last 4 rows until piece measures 54" (137 cm) long, or until you have about 2 yards (2 meters) of yarn left.

Bind off all sts loosely in rib pattern. Weave in ends.

CHILDREN'S COTTON HATS

Kim Hamlin, one of my amazingly creative employees, left Purl one night with a skein of Mission Falls 1824 Cotton, and returned the next morning with the prototype for the hats shown here. She worked the knitted cord into the design so that babies wouldn't be able to fling the hat off. I like the earthy, soft, nubby texture of this yarn.

FINISHED SIZE
To fit baby (toddler, child)

FINISHED MEASUREMENTS
Hat circumference 15 (17½, 20)" (38 [44.5, 51] cm), and hat height 5 (5¼, 5¾)" (12.5 [13.5, 14.5] cm) with brim rolled up.

YARN
Mission Falls 1824 Cotton (100% cotton; 84 yards [77 meters] / 50 grams): 1 skein. Shown in #201 coral (baby), #209 maize (toddler), and #204 lentil (child).

NEEDLES
One 12 (16, 16)" or 30 (40, 40) cm circular needle size US 7 (4.5 mm).
One set of five double-pointed needles size US 7 (4.5 mm). Change needle size if necessary to obtain the correct gauge.

NOTIONS
Yarn needle, scissors, stitch marker.

GAUGE
16 sts and 28 rows = 4" (10 cm) in Stockinette stitch (St st).

Using circular needle, CO (cast on) 60 (70, 80) sts. Join for working in the rnd (round), being careful not to twist, and place marker to indicate the beginning of the rnd. Work in St st (knit all sts every rnd) until hat measures 2" (5 cm) from beginning, with bottom edge unrolled. Work eyelet rnd as follows: K4 (2, 4), *yo, k2tog, k2; repeat from * to end. Work in St st until piece measures 3 (3½, 4)" (7.5 [9, 10] cm) from beginning, with bottom edge unrolled.

Decrease for crown as follows, changing to double-pointed needles when there are too few sts to fit comfortably around the circular needle:
Rnd 1: *K8, k2tog, repeat from * to end—54 (63, 72) sts.
Rnds 2 and 3: Knit.
Rnd 4: *K7, k2tog; repeat from * to end—48 (56, 64) sts.
Rnds 5 and 6: Knit.
Rnd 7: *K6, k2tog; repeat from * to end—42 (49, 56) sts.
Rnds 8 and 9: Knit.
Rnd 10: *K5, k2tog; repeat from * to end—36 (42, 48) sts.
Rnds 11, 13, 15, and 17: Knit.
Rnd 12: *K4, k2tog; repeat from * to end—30 (35, 40) sts.
Rnd 14: *K3, k2tog: repeat from * to end—24 (28, 32) sts.
Rnd 16: *K2, k2tog; repeat from * to end—18 (21, 24) sts.
Rnd 18: *K1, k2tog; repeat from * to end—12 (14, 16) sts.
Rnd 19: K2tog around—6 (7, 8) sts.

Finishing
Break yarn, leaving a 6" (15-cm) tail. With tail threaded on a yarn needle, draw tail through remaining sts and pull snugly to close top of hat. Take tail to inside of hat and fasten securely. Weave in ends.

I-Cord Tie (worked using 2 double-pointed needles)
CO 2 sts onto one double-pointed needle, and k2. Work 2-st I-cord as follows: All Rows: Slide sts to opposite end of needle, bring working yarn around behind the needle and k2. Do not turn work. Keep the same side facing you at all times, and pull the working yarn firmly around behind the sts on the needle to form a knitted tube. Work in this manner until I-cord measures 24 (26, 27)" (61 [66, 68.5] cm), or desired length. Bind off all sts. Weave in ends. Thread I-cord through eyelet holes and tie into a bow in the largest space between eyelets.

KIM'S HATS

Kim Hamlin created this versatile pattern to satisfy the many different tastes and requirements of our customers at Purl. It is also wonderful if you want to make a large assortment of hats as holiday gifts for a group of friends, coworkers, or family members. Pick a collection of yarns that work well together, then use the colors in different ways for each hat. Experiment with different stripes, or add a round of purl stitches occasionally for texture—no two hats alike!

FINISHED SIZE
To fit baby (toddler, child, woman, man)

FINISHED MEASUREMENTS
Hat circumference 14½ (16½, 18½, 20½, 22¾)" (37 [42, 47, 52, 58] cm).

YARN
Manos del Uruguay (100% hand-spun kettle-dyed wool; 137 yards [125 meters] / 100 grams), 1 (1, 1, 1, 2) skeins for earflap hat in a solid color, slightly less for plain hat. See page 63 for the specific colors Kim used.

NEEDLES
One 16" (40-cm) circular needle size US 9 (5.5 mm).
One set of five double-pointed needles size US 9 (5.5 mm).
Change needle size if necessary to obtain the correct gauge.

NOTIONS
Yarn needle, scissors, stitch marker, removable stitch markers.

GAUGE
15½ sts and 23 rows = 4" (10 cm) in Stockinette stitch.

BASIC ROLL BRIM HAT
Using circular needle, cast on 56 (64, 72, 80, 88) sts. Join for working in the rnd (round), being careful not to twist, and place marker to indicate the beginning of the rnd. *Work in Stockinette st (knit all sts every rnd) until hat measures 4¼ (5, 5¾, 6½, 8½)" (11 [12.5, 14.5, 16.5, 21.5] cm) from beginning, or 2½" (6.5 cm) less than desired length, with bottom edge unrolled. Decrease for crown as follows, changing to double-pointed needles when there are too few sts to fit comfortably around the circular needle:

Rnd 1: *K6, k2tog; repeat from * to end—49 (56, 63, 70, 77) sts.
Rnd 2: Knit.
Rnd 3: *K5, k2tog; repeat from * to end—42 (48, 54, 60, 66) sts.
Rnds 4, 5, and 6 and all remaining even-numbered rounds: Knit.
Rnd 7: *K4, k2tog; repeat from * to end—35 (40, 45, 50, 55) sts.
Rnd 9: *K3, k2tog; repeat from * to end—28 (32, 36, 40, 44) sts.
Rnd 11: *K2, k2tog; repeat from * to end—21 (24, 27, 30, 33) sts.
Rnd 13: *K1, k2tog: repeat from * to end—14 (16, 18, 20, 22) sts.

Break yarn, leaving a 6" (15-cm) tail. With tail threaded on a yarn needle, draw tail through remaining sts and pull snugly to close top of hat. Take tail to inside of hat and fasten securely. Weave in ends.

GARTER BRIM VARIATION
Using circular needle, cast on 56 (64, 72, 80, 88) sts. Join for working in the rnd (round), being careful not to twist, and place marker to indicate the beginning of the rnd. Work garter-stitch edging as follows:

Rnd 1: Knit.
Rnd 2: Purl.

Repeat these two rnds until piece measures 1½" (3.8 cm) from beginning. Complete as for Basic Roll Brim Hat, beginning at first * at start of directions.

Helpful Hint:

If possible, measure around the head of the intended recipient, and make the size closest to the head measurement of the wearer. If in between two sizes, make the smaller size.

RIBBED BRIM VARIATION

Using circular needle, cast on 56 (64, 72, 80, 88) sts. Join for working in the rnd (round), being careful not to twist, and place marker to indicate the beginning of the rnd. Work k1, p1 rib as follows:

All Rnds: *K1, p1; repeat from * to end.

Work in k1, p1 rib until piece measures 1½" (3.8 cm) from beginning for a single-layer brim, or 2½" (6.5 cm) for a brim that will be folded up like a cuff. Complete as for Basic Roll Brim Hat, beginning at * at start of directions.

EARFLAP VARIATION

Work as for the Garter Brim Variation until hat measures 5 (5½, 6¼, 7, 9)" (12.5 [14, 16, 18, 23] cm) from beginning, then work crown decreases and finish as for Basic Roll Brim Hat. With a removable marker, mark the center back of hat, between 2 sts. Count forward 6 (6, 8, 8, 10) sts from center back at each side

and place markers. Count forward another 12 (14, 16, 18, 20) sts and place markers again. Remove center back marker. With double-pointed needle and RS facing, pick up and knit 12 (14, 16, 18, 20) sts between one pair of markers, and knit 8 (8, 10, 10 12) rows. On the next row, knit to last 3 sts, end k2tog, k1. Repeat the last row 8 (10, 12, 14, 16) more times—3 sts. On the next row, k2tog, k1—2 sts.

Using the double-pointed needles, work 2-st I-cord as follows for tie:

All Rows: Slide sts to opposite end of needle, bring working yarn around behind the needle and k2. Do not turn work. Keep the same side facing you at all times, and pull the working yarn firmly around behind the sts on the needle to form a knitted tube. Work in this manner until I-cord measures 7 (8, 9, 10, 11)" (18 [20.5, 23, 25.5, 28] cm), or desired length. Bind off all sts. Repeat for other earflap. Weave in ends, using yarn tails at ends of ties to secure pom-poms or tassels, if desired.

Kim used the following colors for the hats shown here and on page 60: #W persimmon, #E English (sage green), #44 briar (purple-taupe), #54 brick, #55 olive, #61 rhubarb, #65 wheat, #47 cerise, #M Bing cherry, #51 jade, #69 hibiscus, #35 uranium (gray-tan), #33 butane (light blue), #49 henna, #20 Parma (light purple).

CASHMERE TEA COZY

This luxurious tea cozy is a great choice for the person on your gift list who already seems to have everything (as long as he or she drinks tea, that is). I chose a stitch pattern that resembles the fabric used to make thermal underwear both because it implies warmth and because, matched with the cashmere yarn, it is such an interesting pairing of luxury and utility. Of course, this cozy can be knit in any worsted-weight wool.

FINISHED MEASUREMENTS
9" (23 cm) high, and 23" (58.5 cm) around at the lower edge.

YARN
Classic Elite Yarns Lavish (100% cashmere; 125 yards [114 meters] / 50 grams): #10033 deep red, 2 skeins.

NEEDLES
One set straight needles size US 8 (5 mm).
Change needle size if necessary to obtain the correct gauge.

NOTIONS
Yarn needle, scissors, removable stitch markers or safety pins, one size US 10 (6 mm) straight needle or needle two sizes larger than main needles for casting on (optional).

GAUGE
15 sts and 26 rows = 4" (10 cm) in textured pattern.

Helpful Hint:
Using the cable cast-on method (see page 132) will make it easier to sew up the seam. If you find it difficult to cast on loosely, use a needle two sizes larger than your main needles for the cast-on. Don't forget to change back to your main needles when you begin knitting.

Loosely cast on 45 sts using the cable cast-on method. Work in textured pattern as follows:
Row 1: (RS) P1, *k1tbl, p1; repeat from * to end.
Row 2: Knit.
Repeat these 2 rows until piece measures 23" (58.5 cm) from beginning, approximately 152 rows. Do not bind off.

Finishing
Thread about a 1-yard (1-meter) length of yarn on a yarn needle. With cozy inside out and WS facing you, join the cast-on edge to the live sts on the needle as follows: Using the tip of the threaded yarn needle, slip first st from knitting needle as if to knit, insert yarn needle tip through first st of cast-on row, pull yarn all the way through to secure. Repeat until all live sts have been joined to the cast-on row. The tea cozy is now in the shape of a cylinder.

Designate one end of cylinder to be the top of tea cozy. With removable stitch markers or safety pins, mark four evenly spaced points along the top edge, (about 38 rows apart if you worked 152 rows). With tea cozy still inside out, bring the four marked points together in the center, and stitch them together securely. There will now be four open sections at the top of the cozy. Turn cozy right side out. Stitch each section closed using mattress stitch (see page 134), working from the center outward. Weave in ends.

Knitted Bobble (optional)
Cast on 1 st, leaving an 8" (20-cm) tail). Knit into front, back, front, back, and then front of same st—5 sts. Purl 1 row, knit 1 row, purl 1 row. On the next row, k5, then pass the second st on right-hand needle over the first, then pass the remaining sts over the first st, one at a time, in order. Break yarn, leaving an 8" (20.5-cm) tail, and pull through last st. Fold bobble with knit side out. Center the bobble in the middle of the top of the cozy, and pull the ends through to the inside of the cozy. Tie securely, and weave in ends.

HAND/WRIST WARMERS

Also called fingerless gloves, these quick-to-knit warmers keep wrists and the upper part of the hands toasty while preserving finger dexterity. In mildly cold weather, they can be worn as is; when it's really cold, they can be layered with gloves underneath. They are shown here in women's and men's versions. The men's pattern is great for all ages, even "cool" teenage boys who worry that handknits might be too girlish for them. One size fits just about everyone, a handy feature for gifts.

WOMEN'S HAND WARMERS

FINISHED SIZE
Will stretch to fit hand sizes up to 8" (20.5 cm) around, about a woman's size large.

FINISHED MEASUREMENTS
Circumference about 6½" (16.5 cm) around (unstretched), and 6½" (16.5 cm) long.

YARN
Noro Cash Iroha (40% silk, 30% lambswool, 20% cashmere, 10% nylon; 100 yards [91 meters] / 40 grams): #84 raspberry, 1 skein.

NEEDLES
Two 8" (20 cm) circular needles size US 6 (4 mm).
Change needle size if necessary to obtain the correct gauge.

NOTIONS
Yarn needle, scissors, stitch marker.

GAUGE
20 sts and 30.5 rows = 4" (10 cm) in spiral rib pattern in the round, with rib relaxed.

Cuff and Lower Hand
Cast on 32 sts onto one circular needle. Join for working in the rnd (round), being careful not to twist, and place marker to indicate the beginning of the rnd. Work in spiral rib pattern as follows:
Rnds 1 - 4: *K2, p2; repeat from * to end.
Rnds 5 - 8: P1, *k2, p2; repeat from * to last 3 sts, end k2, p1.
Rnds 9 - 12: *P2, k2; repeat from * to end.
Rnds 13 - 16: K1, *p2, k2; repeat from * to last 3 sts, end p2, k1.
Work Rnds 1 - 16 a total of two times—32 rows completed; piece measures about 4¼" (11 cm) from beginning.

Thumb Opening
For the next 8 rows, the sts will be worked back and forth to create the thumb opening, using both circular needles as if they were straight needles. The circular needles are necessary to accommodate the curve of the fabric tube you have been working so far. Temporarily remove the end-of-rnd stitch marker while working back and forth.
Row 1: (WS) Using the second circular needle, turn work and *k2, p2; repeat from * to end.
Row 2: (RS) *K2, p2; repeat from * to end.
Rows 3 and 4: Repeat Rows 1 and 2.
Row 5: K1, *p2, k2; repeat from * to last 3 sts, end p2, k1.
Row 6: P1, *k2, p2; repeat from * to last 3 sts, end k2, p1.
Rows 7 and 8: Repeat Rows 5 and 6.

Upper Hand
At end of Row 8, place marker to indicate beginning of rnd, and resume working in the rnd on all sts with the RS of the work facing you as for cuff and lower hand. Work Rnds 9 - 16 of spiral rib pattern once, then work Rnds 1 - 2 once—50 rnds or rows completed; piece measures about 6½" (16.5 cm) from beginning. Bind off all sts in pattern.

Weave in ends.

Make second hand warmer same as the first.

MEN'S HAND WARMERS

FINISHED SIZE
Will stretch to fit hand sizes up to 9" (23 cm) around, about a man's size large.

FINISHED MEASUREMENTS
Circumference about 4½" (11.5 cm) around (unstretched, will appear very skinny), and 8" (20.5 cm) long.

YARN
Koigu Kersti (100% merino wool crepe; 114 yards [104 meters] / 50 grams): #K2420 cocoa brown, 1 skein.

NEEDLES
Two 8" (20 cm) circular needles size US 6 (4 mm).
Change needle size if necessary to obtain the correct gauge.

NOTIONS
Yarn needle, scissors, stitch marker.

GAUGE
36 sts and 30 rows = 4" (10 cm) in k2, p2 rib pattern in the round, with rib relaxed.

Cuff and Lower Hand
Cast on 40 sts onto one circular needle. Join for working in the round (rnd), being careful not to twist, and place marker to indicate the beginning of the rnd. Work in k2, p2 rib pattern as follows:

All Rnds: *K2, p2; repeat from * to end.
Work in k2, p2 rib until piece measures 5¼" (13.5 cm) from beginning, ending the last rnd 1 st before the end of the rnd.

Thumb Opening
For the next 1¾" (4.5 cm), the sts will be worked back and forth in rows to create the thumb opening, using both circular needles as if they were straight needles. The circular needles are necessary to accommodate the curve of the fabric tube you have been working so far. Temporarily remove the end-of-rnd stitch marker while working back and forth. When viewed from the RS, there will be a single purl st at each side of the thumb opening.

Row 1: (WS) K1, *p2, k2; repeat from * to last 3 sts, end p2, k1.
Row 2: (RS) P1, *k2, p2; repeat from * to last 3 sts, end k2, p1.
Repeat these 2 rows 5 more times—12 rows completed; thumb opening measures about 1¾" (4.5 cm) high.

Upper Hand
At end of the last row, purl the first st beyond the thumb opening to rejoin the work in the rnd again, and place marker to indicate beginning of rnd. Resume working in the rnd on all sts with the RS of the work facing you as for cuff and lower hand. Work k2, p2 rib as established until piece measures about 1" (2.5 cm) above the thumb opening, or 8" (20.5 cm) from the beginning. Bind off all sts in pattern.

Weave in ends.

Make second hand warmer same as the first.

AIRY SCARF

This delicate scarf is great if you want to learn the basics of lace knitting. It is also a nice way to use a laceweight mohair on its own without needing magnifying glasses!

When Brenda Overstrom, who teaches at Purl, was designing this romantic piece, we were getting ready for a photo shoot and needed her to finish quickly. She sat down one evening, looked at the clock, and proceeded to knit for four hours, the time limit for patterns in this chapter. Because the scarf she made is relatively small, it is perfect for wearing indoors in places where you desire a little warmth and a little beauty.

FINISHED MEASUREMENTS
6" (15 cm) wide, and 36" (91.5 cm) long.

YARN
Rowan Kidsilk Haze (70% superfine kid mohair, 30% silk; 229 yards [209 meters] / 25 grams): #586 bebe (pale pink), 1 skein.

NOTE:
One skein of this yarn is enough for two scarves.

NEEDLES
One set straight needles size US 10 (6 mm).
Change needle size if necessary to obtain the correct gauge.

NOTIONS
Yarn needle, scissors.

GAUGE
14.5 sts and 18.5 rows = 4" (10 cm) in garter stitch; each eyelet row measures about ¾" (1.9 cm) high.

Cast on 22 sts. Knit 5 rows. Eyelet Row: K1, *k2tog, yo; repeat from * to last st, end k1. Knit 5 rows. *Work Eyelet Row once more. Knit 10 rows. Repeat from * 9 more times—piece measures about 32½" (82.5 cm) from beginning, and end having just completed 10 knit rows. **Work Eyelet Row once more. Knit 5 rows. Repeat from ** one more time. Bind off all sts loosely. Weave in ends. Block.

FOUR-TO-SIX-HOUR GIFTS

CHILD'S PLACKET-NECK PULLOVER

The yarn used for this sweater is Koigu Wool Design's Kersti merino crepe, a lesser-known yarn from the amazing Koigu hand-dyed collection. I think this DK weight yarn is great for projects for babies and young children because it does not itch at all, nor does it shed fibers, and it knits up more quickly than Koigu's thinner yarns. The label recommends working it on size 6 needles at a gauge of 22 stitches and 30 rows to 4 inches, but I personally prefer to knit it a bit more loosely. The looser gauge seems to give a softer, loftier feel to the final piece.

FINISHED SIZE
To fit 0 - 6 months (6 - 12 months, 1 - 2 years, 2 - 4 years, 4 - 6 years, 6 - 8 years, 8 - 10 years).

FINISHED MEASUREMENTS
Chest: 18½ (21, 23, 25, 26, 27, 28)" (47 [53.5, 58.5, 63.5, 66, 68.5, 71] cm).
Length from lower edge to base of neckband: 8½ (10, 11½, 13, 14½, 16, 19)" (21.5 [25.5, 29, 33, 37, 40.5, 48.5] cm.

YARN
Koigu Kersti (100% merino wool crepe; 114 yards [104 meters] / 50 grams): #K2370 gold, 3 (3, 4, 5, 5, 6, 7) skeins.

NEEDLES
One 24" (60-cm) circular needle size US 7 (4.5 mm).
Set of five double-pointed needles size US 7 (4.5 mm).
Change needle size if necessary to obtain the correct gauge.

NOTIONS
Yarn needle, scissors, four stitch markers (one in contrasting color), stitch holders, three beads or buttons approximately ¼" (6 mm) in diameter.

GAUGE
21 sts and 32 rows = 4" (10 cm) in Stockinette stitch.

Lower Body
Cast on 99 (113, 123, 133, 139, 143, 149) sts on circular needle and pm (place marker) to indicate the beginning of the rnd (round). Join for working in the rnd, being careful not to twist sts. Work in seed st as follows:
Rnd 1: *K1, p1; repeat from * to last st, end kl.
Rnd 2: *P1, k1; repeat from * to end to last st, end pl.
Repeat these 2 rnds 3 more times—8 rnds total.
Change to St st (Stockinette st) and work until piece measures 5¼ (6¼, 7¼, 8¼, 9¼, 10, 12¼)" (13.5 [16, 18.5, 21, 23.5, 25.5, 31] cm) from beginning, including seed st edging. On the next rnd, k4 (4, 4, 4, 5, 5, 5), place the last 8 (8, 8, 8, 10, 10, 10) sts worked on a stitch holder, removing the marker for end of rnd from the middle of these sts; k42 (49, 54, 59, 60, 62, 65) for back; k8 (8, 8, 8, 10, 10, 10), and place the last 8 (8, 8, 8, 10, 10, 10) sts on a holder, k41 (48, 53, 58, 59, 61, 64) to end for front. Leave sts on circular needle and set aside.

Sleeves (make 2)
Using dpn (double-pointed needle), cast on 31 (33, 37, 39, 43, 47, 47) sts. Join for working in the rnd, being careful not to twist, and place marker to indicate the beginning of the rnd. Work in seed st as follows:
Rnd 1: *K1, p1; repeat from * to last st, end k1.
Rnd 2: *P1, k1; repeat from * to last st, end p1.
Repeat these 2 rnds 3 more times—8 rnds total.
Change to St st and knit 8 (8, 8, 8, 8, 6, 4) rnds.
Increase Rnd: K1, kf&b (knit into front and back of same st to increase 1 st), knit to last st, kf&b—2 sts increased. Increase 1 st at each end of sleeve in this manner every 8 (8, 8, 8, 7, 6, 4) rnds 1 (2, 3, 4, 5, 7, 11) more time(s)—35 (39, 45, 49, 55, 63, 71) sts. Work even in St st, if necessary, until sleeve measures 4½ (5½, 6½, 7½, 8½, 9, 9½)" (11.5 [14, 16.5, 19, 21.5, 23, 24] cm) from beginning, including seed st cuff. On the next rnd, k4 (4, 4, 4, 5, 5, 5), place the last 8 (8, 8, 8, 10, 10, 10) sts worked on a stitch holder, removing the marker for end of rnd from the middle of these sts, k27 (31, 37, 41, 45, 53, 61) sts to end.
Break yarn.

After working the first sleeve, place marker onto the circular needle, knit the sleeve sts onto the circular needle for the body next to the 41 (48, 53, 58, 59, 61, 64) sts for front, place marker, then knit the back sts. Set aside. You can then use the dpn's to make the second sleeve without having to switch the first sleeve sts from needles to stitch holder and back again.

Make a second sleeve the same as the first, leaving sts on the dpn's.

Yoke

Place marker onto circular needle. Knit 27 (31, 37, 41, 45, 53, 61) sts from dpn for left sleeve onto circular needle next to the sts for back, place marker, k41 (48, 53, 58, 59, 61, 64) for front—137 (159, 181, 199, 209, 229, 251) sts. Place marker for new beginning of rnd, which begins at front right raglan line. Use a different color marker to indicate the beginning of the rnd. Knit 2 rnds even, end last rnd 2 sts before beginning marker. Decrease Rnd: *Ssk, slip marker k1, k2tog, knit to within 2 sts of next marker; repeat from * 3 more times—8 sts decreased, 1 plain knit st between each set of paired decreases along raglan line. Knit 1 rnd even. Repeat the last 2 rnds 1 (2, 3, 3, 3, 5, 7) more time(s), ending the last rnd 21 (24, 25, 28, 28, 27, 27) sts before end of rnd—121 (134, 149, 167, 177, 181, 187) sts: 37 (42, 45, 50, 51, 49, 48) sts for front, 38 (43, 46, 51, 52, 50, 49) sts for back, and 23 (25, 29, 33, 37, 41, 45) sts for each sleeve. Yoke measures about ¾ (1, 1¼, 1¼, 1¼, 1¾, 2¼)" (1.9 [2.5, 3.2, 3.2, 3.2, 4.5, 5.5] cm) above joining rnd.

Neck Placket

Turn work, and use the cable cast-on method (see page 132) to cast on 5 sts at the beginning of the rnd—126 (139, 154, 172, 182, 186, 192) sts. For the placket section of the yoke, you will be working back and forth in rows, continuing the raglan decreases, and working 5 sts at each end of row in seed st as given below.

Seed st over an odd number of sts: On both RS and WS rows [k1, p1] 2 times, k1.

Placket Row 1: (WS) Work 5 sts seed st, purl to last 5 sts, work to end in seed st. Placket Row 2: (RS) Work 5 sts seed st, knit to within 2 sts of next marker, *ssk, slip marker, k1, k2tog, knit to within 2 sts of next marker; repeat from * 3 more times, knit to last 5 sts, work to end in seed st—8 sts decreased.

Repeat these 2 rows 8 (9, 11, 13, 14, 14, 14) more times—54 (59, 58, 60, 62, 66, 72) sts. Work even, without decreasing until work measures 3¼ (3¾, 4¼, 4¾, 5¼, 6, 6¾)" (8.5 [9.5, 11, 12, 13.5, 15, 17] cm) above joining rnd, ending with a WS row.

Neckband

Next row: Work 1 row in Seed st *kl, pl; repeat from * to last st, end k1, AND AT THE SAME TIME decrease 1(0,1,1,1,1,1) st somewhere in the St st section, in order to have an odd number of sts so Seed st at front edges can continue uninterrupted. Work even in seed st for 7 more rows. Bind off all sts in pattern.

Finishing

Using Kitchener st (see page 137), graft underarm sts together. Sew cast-on sts for left placket to base of right placket on the WS, with left placket on top of right placket as in diagram. Sew three beads to right front placket for buttons, with the lowest 1" (2.5 cm) above base of placket, the highest ½" (1.3 cm) down from bound-off edge, and remaining bead centered in between. The beads can be pushed through the sts on the left placket, without stretching the sts, to button the placket. Weave in ends.

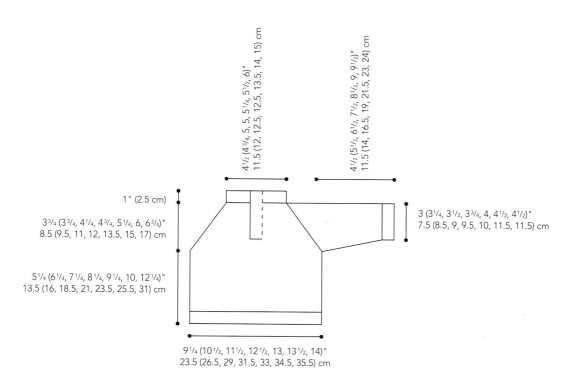

4½ (4¾, 5, 5, 5¼, 5½, 6)"
11.5 (12, 12.5, 12.5, 13.5, 14, 15) cm

4½ (5½, 6½, 7½, 8½, 9, 9½)"
11.5 (14, 16.5, 19, 21.5, 23, 24) cm

1" (2.5 cm)

3¾ (3¾, 4¼, 4¾, 5¼, 6, 6¾)"
8.5 (9.5, 11, 12, 13.5, 15, 17) cm

3 (3¼, 3½, 3¾, 4, 4½, 4½)"
7.5 (8.5, 9, 9.5, 10, 11.5, 11.5) cm

5¼ (6¼, 7¼, 8¼, 9¼, 10, 12¼)"
13.5 (16, 18.5, 21, 23.5, 25.5, 31) cm

9¼ (10½, 11½, 12½, 13, 13½, 14)"
23.5 (26.5, 29, 31.5, 33, 34.5, 35.5) cm

BABY'S DENIM DRAWSTRING PANTS

I've always been intrigued by Rowan's Denim yarn, which is made to shrink and fade in the washing machine and soften with age, just like real jeans, but I have found that many customers are hesitant to trust it to shrink to the right proportions. I can vouch for this yarn's trustworthiness based on my own success with it, but, just to be safe, I've designed these adorable pants so that even if they were to shrink more or less than they should (which they won't!), they are still likely to fit most babies.

FINISHED SIZE
To fit 3-6 months (6-12 months, 12-18 months). See Finished Measurements on page 78.

YARN
Rowan Denim (100% cotton; 101 yards [92 meters] / 50 grams): #229 Memphis, 3 (4, 5) skeins. If you want to use a different yarn that does not shrink like Denim, select one that knits at a gauge of 20 sts = 4" (10 cm), and follow the after-washing lengths shown on the schematic on page 78.

NEEDLES
One 12" (30-cm) and 16" (40-cm) circular needle size US 6 (4 mm). Set of five double-pointed needles size US 6 (4 mm). Change needle size if necessary to obtain the correct gauge.

NOTIONS
Yarn needle, scissors, stitch markers, stitch holder, safety pin or bodkin for inserting drawstring, 1 yard (1 meter) smooth cotton scrap yarn in a contrasting color.

GAUGE
Before washing: 20 sts and 28 rows = 4" (10 cm) in Stockinette stitch; after washing: 20 sts and 32 rows = 4" (10 cm) in Stockinette st.

Legs (make 2)

Using double-pointed needles, cast on 41 (45, 53) sts. Join for working in the rnd (round), being careful not to twist, and place marker to indicate the beginning of the rnd. Work in seed st as follows:
Rnd 1: *K1, p1; repeat from * to last st, end k1.
Rnd 2: *P1, k1; repeat from * to last st, end p1.
Repeat these 2 rnds 3 more times—8 rnds total.
Change to Stockinette st and work until piece measures 9¼ (9¾, 10¼)" (23.5 [25, 26] cm) from beginning, including seed st cuff. Place all sts on holder. Make a second leg the same as the first, leaving sts on the needles, and do not cut yarn.

Join Legs

With 16" (40-cm) circular needle, knit across 21 (23, 27) sts of leg on the needles, cast on 5 sts using the cable cast-on method (see page 132), transfer sts of the second leg from holder to 12" (30-cm) circular needle and knit 41 (45, 53) sts of second leg, cast on 5 sts using the cable cast-on method, knit remaining 20 (22, 26) sts of first leg—92 (100, 116) sts, all on 16" (40-cm) circular needle. Join for working in the rnd, and place marker to indicate new beginning of rnd at side of pants.

Diaper Area

Work in Stockinette stitch until piece measures 6½ (7½, 8¾)" (16.5 [19, 22] cm) above sts cast on for joining legs. Make hole for drawstring as follows: K21 (23, 27), bind off 3 sts at center front, knit to end. On the following rnd, cast on 3 sts using the cable cast-on method above gap in the previous rnd to complete the drawstring hole. Knit 3 more rnds—piece measures about 7 (8, 9¼)" (18 [20.5, 23.5] cm) above sts cast on for joining legs. Purl the next rnd for drawstring casing turning rnd. Knit 8 rnds. Do not bind off.

Waistband

Before sewing down the live stitches, run a piece of scrap cotton through the purl loops along the rnd of sts 9 rnds below the turning rnd; this will make it much easier to attach the live sts in a straight line to keep the waistband even. The facing of the waistband has 8 rnds above the turning rnd, plus the rnd

Before washing: 18 (20, 23)"
(45.5 [51, 58.5] cm) hip circumference, 16 (17¾, 19½)" (40.5
[45, 49.5] cm) long from bottom
of cuffs to top of finished waistband, and 9¼ (9¾, 10¼)" (23.5
[25, 26] cm) inseam length with
cuff unfolded.
After washing: 18 (20, 23)" (45.5
[51, 58.5] cm) hip circumference,
14 (15½, 17)" (35.5 [39.5, 43] cm)
long from bottom of cuffs to
top of finished waistband, and
8 (8½, 9)" (20.5 [21.5, 23] cm)
inseam length with cuff unfolded.

represented by the sts on the needle. Count the loops picked up on the scrap
yarn. In an ideal world, there should be one loop for each live st on the needle.
Typically, I find that I usually have a few too many, or a few too few. If this is the
case, you can "cheat" a bit by joining 2 sts at a time from the knitting needle
(if you picked up too few loops), or skipping a couple of the loops on the scrap
yarn (if you picked up too many). Just make sure to space these adjustments
evenly, and they should not be noticeable when you are finished.

Cut the working yarn, leaving a tail about 3 times the length of the measurement
around the top of the pants. Turn pants inside out and fold the waistband to
the inside along the turning rnd. Holding the waistband smoothly folded down,
join the live sts on the needle to the inside of the pants as follows: Using the
tip of the threaded yarn needle, slip first st from knitting needle as if to knit,
insert yarn needle tip through the purl bump of the st closest to the live st, pull
yarn all the way through to secure, pulling out scrap yarn as you go. Repeat
until all live sts have been joined, making sure to join to the same rnd of the pants
all the way around so the waistband will be even. Cut yarn and secure last st.

I-Cord Drawstring (worked using 2 dpn)
Cast on 2 sts onto one dpn, and k2. Work 2-st I-cord as follows:
All Rows: Slide sts to opposite end of needle, bring working yarn around behind
the needle and k2. Do not turn work. Keep the same side facing you at all times,
and pull the working yarn firmly around behind the sts on the needle to form
a knitted tube. Work in this manner until I-cord measures 32 (36, 40)" (81.5 [91.5,
101.5] cm) or desired length. Bind off all sts.

Finishing
Weave in ends. Wash garment and drawstring cord in hot water, then tumble-
dry on hot setting. Sew extension between legs closed using cast-off to cast-off
method. With a safety pin or bodkin, thread drawstring through waistband and
tie in front. Turn up seed st cuffs, if desired.

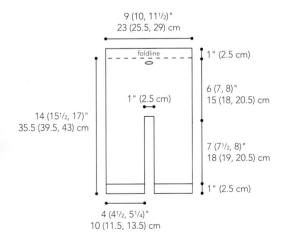

9 (10, 11½)"
23 (25.5, 29) cm

foldline

1" (2.5 cm)

6 (7, 8)"
15 (18, 20.5) cm

1" (2.5 cm)

14 (15½, 17)"
35.5 (39.5, 43) cm

7 (7½, 8)"
18 (19, 20.5) cm

1" (2.5 cm)

4 (4½, 5¼)"
10 (11.5, 13.5) cm

Schematic shows measurements after washing.

MEN'S CASHMERE SCARF

The cashmere used to make this scarf is one of the most beautiful and luxurious available. At Purl we call it "boyfriend yarn" because it comes in many rich, masculine colors and is guaranteed not to itch.

FINISHED MEASUREMENTS
7" (18 cm) wide, and 50"
(127 cm) long.

YARN
Classic Elite Yarns Forbidden
(100% cashmere; 65 yards
[59 meters] / 50 grams): #10065
dark brown, 3 skeins.

NEEDLES
One set straight needles size
US 11 (8 mm).
Change needle size if necessary
to obtain the correct gauge.

NOTIONS
Yarn needle, scissors.

GAUGE
15½ sts and 16 rows = 4"
(10 cm) in pattern stitch.

When joining new skeins of yarn in this project, don't join the new yarn at the edge. If you join the yarns a few sts in, the edges of the scarf will look more tidy.

Cast on 21 sts. Work in pattern st as follows:

Row 1: (WS) *K1, p1; repeat from * to last st, end k1.
Row 2: Knit.
Repeat these 2 rows until there is just enough yarn left for binding off (about 1 yard [1 meter]), ending with Row 1. Bind off all sts loosely as if to knit. Weave in ends.

THE PURL SCARF

The rich, layered beauty of this scarf is created by knitting with two or three strands of yarn together, each strand in a related color, but having a contrasting texture. We call this the Purl Scarf because it has inspired so many of our customers to create scarves in the same style with their own unique yarn combinations. If mixing color on your own makes you nervous, try this: Select a color of Manos Del Uruguay 100% handspun wool, one shade more vibrant than you normally would, then select a thick mohair in a similar, yet slightly more earthy tone. Put these together with a laceweight mohair in a slightly warmer or cooler color than the combination of the other two.

FINISHED MEASUREMENTS
4" to 5" (10 to 12.5 cm) wide, and about 104" (264 cm) long, with rib unstretched, not including fringe.

YARN
About 230 yards (210 meters) each of a bulky yarn and two different mohair yarns.

Shown in:
VENETIAN RED SCARF
Manos del Uruguay (100% hand-spun kettle-dyed wool; 137 yards [125 meters] / 100 grams): #49 henna, 2 skeins.
Rowan Kidsilk Haze (70% superfine kid mohair, 30% silk; 229 yards [209 meters] / 25 grams): #596 marmalade, 1 skein.
Plassard Flore (75% kid mohair, 20% wool, 5% nylon; 100 yards [91 meters] / 50 grams): #106 dark red, 2 skeins.

CELADON SCARF (see page 70)
Manos del Uruguay (100% hand-spun kettle-dyed wool; 137 yards [125 meters] / 100 grams): #18 mint, 2 skeins.
Madil Kid Seta (70% superfine kid mohair, 30% silk; 230 yards [210 meters] / 25 grams): #464 souffle and #725 lime, 1 skein each.

NEEDLES
One set straight needles size US 15 (10 mm). Change needle size if necessary to obtain the correct gauge.

NOTIONS
Yarn needle, scissors, crochet hook size J/10 (6 mm) for applying fringe.

GAUGE
Venetian Red Scarf: 13½ sts and 8½ rows = 4" (10 cm) in k1, p1 rib pattern.

Celadon Scarf: 16 sts and 9½ rows = 4" (10 cm) in k1, p1 rib pattern.

Exact gauge is not critical for this project.

NOTE:
If you decide to create your own blend of yarns (which I hope you will!), matching the gauge of the scarves shown here is not crucial. However, if your yarn is much bulkier than the red scarf, you may want to cast on fewer stitches because with bulky yarns a too-wide scarf can be uncomfortable. Whatever yarn you use, be sure to cast on an even number of stitches so that the pattern will work properly.

Holding all three strands together, cast on 16 sts. Work in k1, p1 rib pattern as follows:

All Rows: *K1, p1; repeat from * to end.
Repeat this row until scarf is about 104" (264 cm) long. Bind off all sts in rib pattern.

Weave in ends.

Fringe
The fringe on the Venetian Red Scarf is made with the Manos del Uruguay color #49 and Rowan Kidsilk Haze color #596; the fringe on the Celadon Scarf is made with all three strands used in the scarf.

To make fringe, hold the strands that you will use in the fringe together, and wrap them around something about 8" (20 cm) wide (such as a book). Cut the strands across the bottom to create a bundle of 16" (40.5-cm) lengths. Use crochet hook to pull the loops at the center of the fringe bundle through the first knit st at one end of the scarf, then pass the cut ends through the loop and pull snugly. Continue in this manner, applying fringe to every other st, until all 8 knit sts at each end of the scarf have a fringe. Trim the ends of the fringe even.

MEN'S RUSTIC SCARF

This scarf is made with a wonderfully earthy, tweed wool yarn that has a rugged, rustic look, but is not at all itchy. The colors of the stripes are rich but not too bright, which I've observed is the usual preference of the men whom I meet at Purl. Because you cast on stitches for the full length of the scarf, the stripes are vertical, rather than the typical horizontal stripes for scarves. Because you are working an odd number of rows for each garter stitch stripe, "blips" of the old color are introduced at the beginning of a stripe in a new color. This adds an unexpected modern touch.

FINISHED MEASUREMENTS
6" (15 cm) wide and 62" (157.5 cm) long.

YARN
Rowan Yorkshire Tweed Chunky (100% wool; 109 yards [100 meters] / 100 grams): #554 stout (dark brown, A), #557 olive oil (B), and #551 string (tan, C), 1 skein each.

NEEDLES
One 40" (100-cm) circular needle size US 11 (8 mm). Change needle size if necessary to obtain the correct gauge.

NOTIONS
Yarn needle, scissors.

GAUGE
11 sts and 24 rows (12 garter ridges) = 4" (10 cm) in garter stitch.

With color A, loosely cast on 171 sts, and knit 9 rows. Change to color B and knit 9 rows. Change to color C and knit 9 rows. Change to color B and knit 3 rows. Change to color A and knit 3 rows.

Bind off all sts loosely with color A, matching the tension of the cast-on so the long sides of the scarf will be even. If you find it difficult to bind off loosely, try working the bind-off row with a larger needle, such as a US 13 (9 mm) or 15 (10 mm). On a project like this a too-tight bind-off will create a ridged edge that pulls the scarf out of shape and prevents it from feeling supple and comfortable.

Weave in ends.

SOFT DRAWSTRING POUCH

I love that this project is both a gift in itself as well as a gift wrapping. It could beautifully hold a skein of handspun cashmere, a jewelry box, a handknit baby hat, or the Silk Camisole on page 96. The yarn is a lovely blend of alpaca and silk, which gives the pouch a soft, luscious drape and a lustrous sheen.

FINISHED MEASUREMENTS
5 (6¾, 8)" (12.5 [17, 20.5] cm) wide, and 8 (9, 10)" (20.5 [23, 25.5] cm) high, with top edge slightly rolled.

YARN
Blue Sky Alpacas Alpaca and Silk (50% superfine alpaca, 50% silk; 146 yards [134 meters] / 50 grams): 1 (1, 2) skeins.

Shown #110 ecru (small), #116 spring (green, medium), and #113 ice (blue, large).

NEEDLES
One 16" (40 cm) circular needle size US 6 (4 mm).
Two double-pointed needles size US 6 (4 mm).
Change needle size if necessary to obtain the correct gauge.

NOTIONS
Yarn needle, scissors, stitch marker, crochet hook size F/6 (4 mm) for applying fringe.

GAUGE
24 sts and 28 rows = 4" (10 cm) in Stockinette stitch.

Using circular needle, cast on 90 (120, 144) sts. Join for working in the rnd (round), being careful not to twist, and place marker to indicate the beginning of the rnd. Work in Stockinette st (knit all sts every rnd) until piece measures 3" (7.5 cm) from beginning. Eyelet Rnd: *Yo, slip 1, k2tog, pass slipped st over; repeat from * to end—60 (80, 96) sts. Work in Stockinette st until piece measures 6 (7, 8)" (15 [18, 20.5] cm) from Eyelet Rnd.

Finishing
Turn pouch inside out. Fold the circular needle in half and divide stitches equally between each half. Using a single double-pointed needle as the working needle, join the two halves with a three-needle bind-off (see page 133). Weave in loose ends. Turn pouch right side out.

I-Cord Tie (worked using 2 double-pointed needles)
Cast on 2 sts onto one double-pointed needle, and k2.
Work 2-st I-cord as follows:
All Rows: Slide sts to opposite end of needle, bring working yarn around behind the needle and k2. Do not turn work. Keep the same side facing you at all times, and pull the working yarn firmly around behind the sts on the needle to form a knitted tube. Work in this manner until I-cord measures 12 (14, 16)" (30.5 [35.5, 40.5] cm) or desired length. Bind off all sts. Weave in ends.

Fringe
Cut five 5" (12.5-cm) strands of yarn, and fold the bundle of strands in half. Use crochet hook to pull the loops at the top of the fold through the end st of the I-cord tie, then pass the cut ends through the loop and pull snugly. Cut a 12" to 16" (30.5- to 40.5-cm) strand of yarn, align one end with the bottom of the cut ends of the fringe. Beginning about 1" (2.5 cm) above top of the fringe, wrap the yarn downwards for 1" (2.5 cm), just covering the join between the cord and fringe. Thread the end of the wrapping yarn on a yarn needle, and run the end back up through the wrap, then down through the end of the wrap, and out to end the fringe. Trim even with fringe ends. Make second fringe at the other end of the I-cord tie.

Beginning and ending at the center front of pouch, thread I-cord through eyelet holes. Fill the pouch with something wonderful, cinch the cord, and tie at center front.

GUSSETED FLOOR CUSHIONS

In my small New York apartment I use a lot of floor cushions for seating because they're easy to stack and put away when not in use, and they create a casually intimate atmosphere when friends come over (and they give my friends a place to sit instead of the floor). These are knit quite tightly in a very bulky hand-dyed alpaca yarn that I love. I chose reverse stockinette stitch for them as soon as I saw how modern and pebble-like the stitches looked in this yarn and pattern. They make a great gift for a new home with an urban feeling.

FINISHED MEASUREMENTS
About 18" (45.5 cm) square, and 4" (10) thick.

YARN
Blue Sky Alpacas Bulky Hand Dyes (50% alpaca, 50% wool; 45 yards [41 meters] / 100 grams): #1016 gold, 10 skeins.

NEEDLES
One 24" (60-cm) circular needle size US 15 (10 mm). Change needle size if necessary to obtain the correct gauge.

NOTIONS
Yarn needle, scissors, crochet hook size K/10½ (6.5 mm) for edging, extra-firm foam block cut to 18" (45.5 cm) square and 4" (10 cm) thick.

GAUGE
9 sts and 13 rows = 4" (10 cm) in reverse Stockinette stitch.

NOTE:
Since the sides of the cushion measure 4" (10 cm), skip the gauge swatch; just start knitting one of the vertically-worked sides and use it to check your gauge. If your gauge is correct, continue knitting; if not, begin again with a different-size needle.

Vertically-Worked Sides (make 2)
Cast on 9 sts. Work in reverse Stockinette st (rev St st) with Stockinette st (St st) selvedges as follows:
Row 1: (WS): P1, knit to last st, p1.
Row 2: (RS): K1, purl to last st, k1.
Repeat these 2 rows until 58 rows have been completed, ending with a wrong-side row—piece measures about 18" (45.5 cm) from beginning. Bind off all sts loosely as if to knit.

Horizontally-Worked Sides (make 2)
Cast on 40 sts. Work in rev St st with St st selvedges as for the vertically-worked sides until 13 rows have been completed, ending with a wrong-side row—piece measures about 4" (10 cm) from beginning. Bind off all sts loosely as if to knit.

Top and Bottom (make 2)
Cast on 40 sts. Work in rev St st with St st selvedges as for the sides until 58 rows have been completed, ending with a wrong-side row—piece measures about 18" (45.5 cm) from beginning. Bind off all sts loosely as if to knit.

Finishing
When crocheting the pieces together, match the stitches and rows, one-for-one. This will make the finishing easier and neater. The cushion is assembled from the outside (purl side facing out) using a crocheted slip stitch (see page 136). Being sure to match the corners carefully, use the crochet hook to slipstitch the bound-off edge of top to the bound-off edge of a horizontally-worked side. Continue around the top, and join one of the selvedges of top and a vertically-worked side. Continue across the cast-on edge of the top, joining the cast-on edge to the cast-on edge of the other horizontally-worked side. For the last side, join the remaining selvedge edge of top to the selvedge edge of the other vertically-worked side. Insert the foam block into the partially-assembled cushion. Place the bottom over the foam, and rotate it, if necessary, so that you can join sts to sts, and rows to rows, just as for the other pieces. Slipstitch around all 4 sides as before to complete the cushion. Weave in ends.

SIX-TO-EIGHT-HOUR GIFTS

CIRCLE OF FRIENDS GARTER-STITCH BLANKET

This blanket is knit entirely in garter stitch in seven strips of seven colors. Although one person can certainly knit this blanket all by him or herself, my idea in designing it was for a circle of friends (or family members) to collaborate and knit it for the newborn child of someone close to all of them. In order to make this blanket in a hurry, it is best knit by seven people, each doing one strip that will later be sewn together by the quickest finisher in the bunch. With everyone working on it at once, it's sure to be ready on time!

FINISHED MEASUREMENTS
36" (91.5 cm) square.

YARN
Rowan Wool Cotton (50% wool, 50% cotton; 123 yards [112 meters] / 50 grams): #900 antique (cream, A), #950 mango (orange, B), #947 spark (paprika, C), #911 rich (red, D), #910 gypsy (wine, E), #944 tulip (purple, F), and #952 hiss (lavender, G), 2 skeins each.

NEEDLES
One set straight needles size US 6 (4 mm).
Change needle size if necessary to obtain the correct gauge.

NOTIONS
Yarn needle, scissors.

GAUGE
20 sts and 34 rows (17 garter ridges) = 4" (10 cm) in garter stitch.

With the first color for your strip (see color sequences below), cast on 25 sts and knit every row for 44 rows (22 garter ridges). Change to the next color, and knit 44 rows. Leave long tails when switching colors so they can be used to sew the strips together. Continue in this manner, knitting 44 rows of each color, in order, until you have a strip seven blocks high. Bind off all sts.

Color Sequences
Strip 1: A, B, C, D, E, F, G
Strip 2: G, A, B, C, D, E, F
Strip 3: F, G, A, B, C, D, E
Strip 4: E, F, G, A, B, C, D
Strip 5: D, E, F, G, A, B, C
Strip 6: C, D, E, F, G, A, B
Strip 7: B, C, D, E, F, G, A

Finishing
Arrange strips as shown below (cast-on edge of each strip is at the bottom of the diagram). Sew seams. Weave in ends.

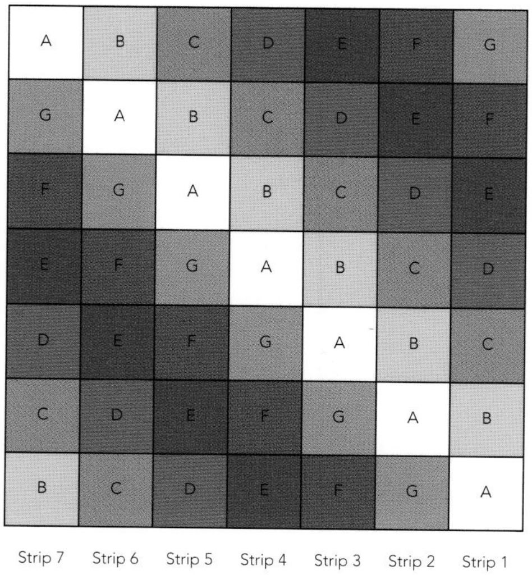

Strip 7 Strip 6 Strip 5 Strip 4 Strip 3 Strip 2 Strip 1

Each strip begins and ends with a different color, but follows the same color order. This creates a dynamic diagonal pattern that visually integrates each friend's strip into the others.

FELTED YOGA MAT BAG

I know a lot of people who practice yoga (quite a few are knitters), and I'm sure many of them would choose this pretty, all-natural bag for carrying their yoga mat over the nylon kind sold at most sporting-goods stores. The wool yarn used in this project comes from a cooperative that supports over a thousand Uruguayans, mostly rural women.

FINISHED MEASUREMENTS
16" (40.5 cm) circumference, 24" (61 cm) long, with 40" (101.5 cm) strap.

YARN
Manos del Uruguay (100% handspun kettle-dyed wool; 137 yards [125 meters] / 100 grams): #01 Hollywood pink (A), 2 skeins; #113 wildflowers (B), 3 skeins; #W persimmon (C), 1 skein.

NEEDLES
One 24" (60 cm) circular needle size US 10½ (6.5 mm). Set of five double-pointed needles size US 10½ (6.5 mm). Change needle size if necessary to obtain the correct gauge.

NOTIONS
Yarn needle, scissors, stitch markers, removable stitch marker or safety pin.

GAUGE
Before washing: 14 sts and 18 rows = 4" (10 cm) in Stockinette stitch.

With A and circular needle, loosely cast on 80 sts. Join for working in the rnd (round), being careful not to twist, and place marker to indicate the beginning of the rnd. *Purl 1 rnd, knit 1 rnd; repeat from * once more—4 rnds completed. Knit 30 rnds—piece measures about 7" (18 cm) from beginning. Note: The fabric will be very loose and stretchy; take care not to pull it too much lengthwise when checking your measurements. Cut A, join B, and knit 34 rnds—piece measures about 14½" (37 cm) from beginning. Cut B, join C, and knit 100 rnds—piece measures about 37" (94 cm) from beginning. Cut C, join A, and knit 36 rnds—piece measures about 45" (114 cm) from beginning.

Bottom
Continuing with A, decrease for bottom of bag as follows, changing to double-pointed needles when there are too few sts to fit comfortably around the circular needle:

Rnd 1: Purl.
Rnd 2: Knit.
Rnd 3: *K6, k2tog; repeat from * to end—70 sts.
Rnd 4 and All Remaining Even-Numbered Rnds: Knit.
Rnd 5: *K5, k2tog tbl; repeat from * to end—60 sts.
Rnd 7: *K4, k2tog; repeat from * to end—50 sts.
Rnd 9: *K3, k2tog tbl; repeat from * to end—40 sts.
Rnd 11: *K2, k2tog; repeat from * to end—30 sts.
Rnd 13: *K1, k2tog tbl; repeat from * to end—20 sts.
Rnd 15: K2tog around—10 sts.
Alternating the type of decreases used makes them less noticeable in the finished bag.

Break yarn, leaving a 6" (15 cm) tail. With tail threaded on a yarn needle, draw tail through remaining sts and pull snugly to close bottom of bag. Take tail to inside of bag and fasten securely. Weave in ends.

Bottom Ridge
This ridge defines the bottom of the bag and adds sturdiness. Slip the circular needle into the top loops of the purl sts of Rnd 1 of the bottom—80 loops on needle. Join A and knit 1 rnd. BO 62 sts—18 live sts remain.

Strap

The strap is worked with a 3-st tubular border at each side; the extra yo that is dropped on the subsequent row adds a little extra firmness to the felted strap and keeps the edge from pulling in. Transfer 18 strap sts to a single double-pointed needle and work back and forth in rows as follows:

Row 1: K15, yo, slip 3 sts as if to purl with yarn in front.
Row 2: Pull the working yarn firmly around behind the slipped sts to form a tubular edge, k3, drop yo from needle, k12, yo, slip 3 sts as if to purl with yarn in front.
Repeat Row 2 until strap measures 47" (119.5 cm). Do not bind off. Cut yarn, leaving an 18" (45.5-cm) tail.

Lay the bag flat with the strap centered on the top layer. Place a removable marker or safety pin at the top edge of the layer underneath, exactly in the center. Smooth the strap all the way to the top of the bag, keeping it centered. Match the middle of the strap to the marker on the under layer, and sew the live sts of the strap to the top of the under layer. Make sure the strap is straight and not twisted so it will be comfortable when worn.

Felting

Set washer for hot wash and medium water lever. Add a small amount (about 1 tablespoon) of Wool Mix (a rinse-free wool wash that is excellent for felting) or a mild liquid detergent.

Before placing the bag in the washer, turn it inside out with the strap inside, and place it in a zippered pillowcase or a fine mesh bag to protect the washing machine from the excess fiber that will be released during felting. After 5 minutes, stop the washer and check the progress of the felting. Remove the bag from the pillowcase so that you can really see how it is doing, paying special attention to the strap, and smoothing out any twists before tucking it inside the bag again. Restart the machine, and continue to check the felting and smooth the strap every 5 minutes. Manos del Uruguay yarn felts quickly, so if you want a perfect bag do not be tempted to skip any of these progress checks! If needed, reset machine to agitate longer. Do not let the machine drain and spin because this may cause permanent creasing of your bag. When the bag is the correct size, remove and rinse by hand if necessary (not required if you used Wool Mix). Use several towels to remove as much water as possible, shape and air-dry away from heat and sunlight. Don't be surprised if the drying time is longer than the knitting time!

PASHMINA COWL

This cowl is made with an extra-fine cashmere yarn that is so soft it belongs right up against the skin. I wear this cowl two different ways depending on my mood: either folded in half so that it stands up around the neck, or unfolded and slouchy. Either way it looks and feels great.

FINISHED MEASUREMENTS
20" (51 cm) circumference, and 13" (33 cm) high with edges rolled.

YARN
Joseph Galler Pashmina I (100% superfine cashmere; 170 yards [155 meters] / 50 grams): musk (taupe), 2 skeins.

NEEDLES
One 16" (40 cm) circular needle size US 5 (3.75 mm).
Change needle size if necessary to obtain the correct gauge.

NOTIONS
Yarn needle, scissors, stitch marker.

GAUGE
26 sts and 38 rows = 4" (10 cm) in Stockinette stitch.

Cast on 130 sts. Join for working in the rnd (round), being careful not to twist, and place marker to indicate the beginning of the rnd. Knit 5 rnds, purl 1 rnd. Work in Stockinette st (knit all sts every rnd) until piece measures 12½" (31.5 cm) from purl rnd. Purl 1 rnd, knit 5 rnds. Bind off all sts loosely as if to knit. Weave in ends.

SILK CAMISOLE

This camisole is made with La Luz, an exquisite handspun, hand-dyed silk from Fiesta Yarns. It feels soft and lovely against the skin and it drapes so beautifully that the camisole doesn't need any waist shaping to make it flattering. The straps are made directly from the top of each side, not sewn on, and then grafted onto stitches along the back, so they are very secure. The picot edge looks delicate at the V-neck but it is also utilitarian because it helps keep the neck in place while wearing. The lace stitch at the bottom of the camisole—a simple nine-stitch repeat—adds an elegant touch and also makes the yarn go further! This camisole looks great worn alone as shown as well as over a silk slip dress or cotton tank top in a complementary color.

FINISHED MEASUREMENTS
Chest: 28 (32, 36, 40, 44)"
(71 [81.5, 91.5, 101.5, 112] cm)
Length from lower edge to underarm: 15½ (15¾, 16, 16½, 17)" (39.5 [40, 40.5, 42, 43] cm).

YARN
Fiesta Yarns La Luz (100% silk; 210 yards [192 meters]/ 2 ounces [57 grams]): wild iris, 2 (3, 3, 4, 4) skeins.

NEEDLES
One 24" (60 cm) circular needle size US 7 (4.5 mm).
Two double-pointed needles size US 5 (3.75 mm).
Change needle size if necessary to obtain the correct gauge.

NOTIONS
Yarn needle, scissors, stitch markers, removable stitch markers or safety pins, stitch holders, crochet hook size E/4 (3.5 mm) for picking up stitches around neck (optional).

GAUGE
24 sts and 26 rows = 4" (10 cm) in Stockinette stitch.

Lower Body
With circular needle, cast on 84 (97, 108, 120, 133) sts, place marker, cast on another 84 (97, 108, 120, 133) sts—168 (194, 216, 240, 266) sts. Join for working in the rnd (round), being careful not to twist, and place marker to indicate the beginning of the rnd.

Work lace border as follows:

Rnd 1: Knit.
Rnd 2: *K1 (3, 4, 1, 3), [k1, yo, k2, ssk, k2tog, k2, yo] 9 (10, 11, 13, 14) times, k2 (4, 5, 2, 4), slip marker; repeat from * once more.
Rnd 3: Knit.
Rnd 4: *K2 (4, 5, 2, 4), [k1, yo, k2, ssk, k2tog, k2, yo] 9 (10, 11, 13, 14) times, k1 (3, 4, 1, 3), slip marker; repeat from * once more.
Repeat these 4 rnds until piece measures 3" (7.5 cm) from beginning. Change to Stockinette stitch (knit all sts every rnd) and work until piece measures 13 (13¼, 13½, 14, 14½)" (33 [33.5, 34.5, 35.5, 37] cm) from beginning, or 2½" (6.5 cm) less than desired length to underarm.

Divide for V-Neck
K42 (48, 54, 60, 66), bind off 0 (1, 0, 0, 1) st(s) at center front, knit to end of rnd, then knit the first 42 (48, 54, 60, 66) sts again—168 (193, 216, 240, 265) sts: 84 (97, 108, 120, 133) sts for back, 42 (48, 54, 60, 66) sts each in two front sections on either side of center front marker. Turn, and begin working back and forth in rows; the ends of each row are at the center front.

Work in rows, decreasing at center front for V-neck as follows:

Row 1: (WS) *K1, purl to 1 st before center front, k1.
Row 2: (RS) *K2, ssk, knit to last 4 sts before center front, k2tog, k2—2 sts

decreased, 1 on each side of center V. Repeat these 2 rows 6 more times, then work Row 1 once more—154 (179, 202, 226, 251) sts: 84 (97, 108, 120, 133) sts for back, 35 (41, 47, 53, 59) sts each in two front sections; piece measures about 15½ (15¾, 16, 16½, 17)" (39.5 [40, 40.5, 42, 43] cm) from beginning.

Bind Off for Back and Underarms

On the next row (RS), k1, ssk, k26 (32, 38, 44, 50), k2tog, k1, bind off 3 sts, remove side marker, bind off 17 (20, 23, 26, 29) sts, k4 and place these 4 sts on holder, bind off center 42 (49, 54, 60, 67) sts of back, k4 and place these 4 sts on holder, bind off 17 (20, 23, 26, 29) sts, remove side marker, bind off 3 sts, k1, ssk, k26 (32, 38, 44, 50), k2tog, k1—30 (36, 42, 48, 54) sts each in two front sections; 4 sts each on two stitch holders for back of straps. Do not break yarn. Leave right front sts on circular needle while working the left front.

Left Front

Turn, and work back and forth in rows on 30 (36, 42, 48, 54) left front sts only.
Row 1: (WS) K1, purl to last st, k1.
Row 2: (RS) K1, ssk, knit to last 3 sts, k2tog, k1—2 sts decreased.
Repeat the last 2 rows until 6 sts remain. Mark both ends of the row to indicate where to pick up sts for picot trim later. On the next row, p1, p2tog twice, p1—4 sts. Slip 4 sts onto a single double-pointed needle with right side facing, and k4.

Work 4-st I-cord strap using 2 double-pointed needles as follows:

All Rows: Slide sts to opposite end of needle, bring working yarn around behind the needle and k4. Do not turn work. Keep the same side facing you at all times, and pull the working yarn firmly around behind the sts on the needle to form a knitted tube. Work in this manner until I-cord measures about 13 (13¼, 13½, 13¾, 14)" (33 [33.5, 34.5, 35, 35.5] cm) pulled taut. Place sts on a holder.

Right Front

Join yarn to 30 (36, 42, 48, 54) sts for right front with wrong side facing, ready to work a wrong side row.
Row 1: (WS) K1, purl to last st, k1.
Row 2: (RS) K1, ssk, knit to last 3 sts, k2tog, k1—2 sts decreased.
Repeat the last 2 rows until 6 sts remain. Mark both ends of the row to indicate where to pick up sts for picot trim later. On the next row, p1, p2tog twice, p1—4 sts. Work I-cord strap as for left front. Place sts on holder.

Finishing

Temporarily pin the ends of the straps to the sts on hold at the top of the back, being careful that none of the live sts escape. Try on camisole, and adjust straps, adding or removing rows to customize the fit. Graft the 4 live sts of each strap to the corresponding 4 live sts on holder at top of the back, using Kitchener st (see page 137).

Neck Trim

This picot neck trim is not only decorative, it is also functional because it reinforces the edge around the V-neck, and helps to improve the fit when wearing the camisole. With RS facing, using crochet hook to assist if desired, beginning at the marked row on the left front neck edge, pick up and knit 33 sts along front V-neck to marked row on right front neck edge (see page 135). Purl 1 row on WS. Work picot bind-off on next row as follows: bind off 2 sts, *slip remaining st back to left-hand needle, cast on 2 sts using the cable cast-on method (see page 132). Bind off 4 sts; repeat from * to end, pull yarn through loop of last st and secure.

Weave in ends. Block lightly, paying particular attention to opening up the lace border.

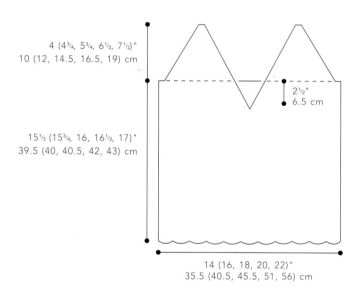

4 (4¾, 5¾, 6½, 7½)"
10 (12, 14.5, 16.5, 19) cm

2½"
6.5 cm

15½ (15¾, 16, 16½, 17)"
39.5 (40, 40.5, 42, 43) cm

14 (16, 18, 20, 22)"
35.5 (40.5, 45.5, 51, 56) cm

CABLED PURSE

This bag was designed by Mary Lou Risely. She and I arranged to meet at Purl one day to discuss ideas, but the store became so busy I only had time to draw a rough sketch and answer a few questions. We briefly acknowledged that the bag needed to be lined but didn't figure out how. A few days later Mary Lou suggested a knitted lining, which I think is perfect because it gives the bag a pulled-together look as well as a soft structure that keeps it from drooping.

FINISHED MEASUREMENTS
5¼" (13.5 cm) wide, and 6" (15 cm) high, with 36" (91.5 cm) long strap.

YARN
Koigu Premium Merino (KPM) (100% Merino wool; 170 yards [155 meters] / 50 grams): #1110 paprika, 1 skein.

NEEDLES
One 12" (30-cm) circular needle size US 3 (3.25 mm).
Two double-pointed needles size US 3 (3.25 mm).
Change needle size if necessary to obtain the correct gauge.

NOTIONS
Yarn needle, scissors, stitch holders, stitch markers.

GAUGE
28 sts and 36 rows = 4" (10 cm) in pattern stitch.

STITCH GUIDE
K1tbl: knit 1 st through the back loop.

Right Twist: K2tog but leave sts on left-hand needle. Insert right-hand needle tip between sts just worked, knit the first st again, then slip both sts from the left-hand needle together.

M5: Make 5 sts from 1 st by working p1, k1, p1, k1, p1 all in same st.

Because this purse is knit in the round and both sides look alike, choose stitch markers of different colors, designating a specific color for the beginning of the round.

Cast on 72 sts on circular needle. Join for working in the rnd (round), being careful not to twist, and place marker to indicate the beginning of the rnd. Knit 36 sts, place marker to indicate side of bag, knit to end—2 markers in bag: one at beginning of rnd, and one at the halfway point.

On the next rnd, work according to Rnd 1 of chart on page 103, slip marker, work Rnd 1 of chart again. Continue in this manner, repeating the chart twice around, until Rnd 54 has been completed—piece measures about 6" (15 cm) from beginning. Note: The number of sts will not stay the same every rnd while you are working the embossed bell motifs.

Turning Rnd: On the next rnd, removing markers as you come to them, purl the first 3 sts and place them on a small stitch holder, purl to next marker, purl the next 3 sts and place them on a small stitch holder, purl to end—66 sts remain, 33 sts each in two groups.

Lining
Knit 1 rnd on 66 sts, skipping over the sts on holders. Work in Stockinette st (knit all sts every rnd) until lining measures 5½" (14 cm) from turning rnd. Fold the circular needle in half and divide stitches equally between each half. Turn lining inside out. Using a single double-pointed needle as the working needle, join the two halves with a three-needle bind-off (see page 133). Weave in loose ends. Turn entire purse right side out, and tuck lining down inside outer shell of purse.

I-Cord Strap (worked using 2 double-pointed needles)

Slip 3 sts from one holder onto a single double-pointed needle, and k3.
Work 3-st I-cord as follows:

All Rows: Slide sts to opposite end of needle, bring working yarn around behind the needle and k3. Do not turn work. Keep the same side facing you at all times, and pull the working yarn firmly around behind the sts on the needle to form a knitted tube. Work in this manner until I-cord measures 36" (91.5 cm). Using Kitchener stitch (see page 137), graft 3 sts of strap to live sts from other holder.

Finishing

Sew bottom seam of bag, tacking lining to bottom edge of bag before closing bottom seam, if desired. Weave in loose ends. Block lightly.

Helpful Hint:

Consider using a Post-It note to keep your place on the chart. I always cover the row above the one I am working, so that I can compare the rows below with what I've already done.

	knit
•	purl
ℑ	k1tbl
5	M5
╱	k2tog
╲	ssk
⅄	sl 1, k2tog, pass slipped st over
⨝	right twist
▨	no stitch

54
53
52
51
50
49
48
47
46
45
44
43
42
41
40
39
38
37
36
35
34
33
32
31
30
29
28
27
26
25
24
23
22
21
20
19
18
17
16
15
14
13
12
11
10
9
8
7
6
5
4
3
2
1

LOVABLE TOYS

I love the old-fashioned charm of these toys, which were designed by Marion Edmonds, who along with her business partner, Ahza Moore, runs a company called Knitting Together NYC. (Ahza created the mini sweater and stocking patterns on page 46). The bear, rabbit, and elephant all share the same body, and variations in the head and ears lend them their distinct personalities. These toys are knit in the round with minimal sewing. Maybe you'll have time to whip up all three!

FINISHED MEASUREMENTS
About 10" (25 cm) tall not including ears, and 8" (20.5 cm) wide from paw to paw.

YARN
Blue Sky Alpacas Sportweight (100% alpaca; 134 yards [123 meters] / 2 ounces [57 grams]: 2 skeins for each toy. Shown in #000 natural white for rabbit, #002 natural copper for bear, and #009 natural light gray for elephant.

This yarn is used doubled throughout.

ADDITIONAL YARN FOR EACH TOY
Rabbit
Belangor French Angora (100% angora; 33 yards [30 meters] / 10 grams): #802 pink for inner ears, 1 skein.
Scraps of pink and light blue yarn or embroidery floss for mouth and eyes.

Bear
Blue Sky Alpacas Sportweight (100% alpaca; 134 yards [123 meters] / 2 ounces [57 grams]: #211 paprika for scarf, 1 skein.
Scraps of dark brown and light blue yarn or embroidery floss for mouth and eyes.

Elephant
Blue Sky Alpacas Alpaca and Silk (50% superfine alpaca, 50% silk; 146 yards [134 meters] / 50 grams): #133 blush (light pink) for kerchief and tip of nose.
Scraps of blue yarn or embroidery floss for eyes.

NEEDLES
Two 24" (60-cm) circular needles size US 6 (4 mm).
Set of five double-pointed needles size US 6 (4 mm) for elephant trunk.
Change needle size if necessary to obtain the correct gauge.

NOTIONS
Yarn needle, scissors, stitch markers, removable stitch markers or safety pins, stitch holders, smooth cotton scrap yarn for provisional cast-on, crochet hook size G/7 (4.5 mm) for provisional cast-on, polyester fiberfill or wool for stuffing.

GAUGE
18 sts and 30 rows = 4" (10 cm) in Stockinette stitch with doubled strand of main yarn.

STITCH GUIDE
Make 1 (M1): Insert the left-hand needle tip underneath the strand between the two needles from front to back. Knit the lifted strand through its back loop, twisting it to avoid leaving a hole.

Arms (make 2)

With doubled strand of main yarn, cast on 18 sts. Working back and forth in rows, and beginning with a purl row, work 15 rows in Stockinette st (knit all sts on RS [right side]; purl all sts on WS [wrong side]). On the next row (RS), k2tog all the way across—9 sts. Cut yarn, leaving a 12" (30.5-cm) tail. With tail threaded on a yarn needle, draw tail through remaining sts and pull snugly to close end of paw. Take tail to inside of arm and fasten securely. Use mattress stitch (see page 134) to sew arm seam, leaving top of arm open for stuffing later. Weave in ends. Make a second arm the same as the first.

Legs (make 2)

With doubled strand of main yarn, cast on 10 sts. Working back and forth in rows, work as follows:
Row 1: (RS) Kf&b (knit in front and back of st to increase 1 st) all the way across—20 sts.
Rows 2 and 3: Knit.
Rows 4 - 18: Work in Stockinette st, beginning and ending with a purl row. Leave sts on needle, cut yarn, and set aside. Using the other circular needle, make a second leg the same as the first.

Body

Redistribute the sts on the two circular needles as follows: With RS facing, place the last 10 sts of the second leg and the first 10 st of the first leg on one needle, then place the remaining 10 sts of the first leg and the first 10 sts of the second leg on the other needle. Half the sts for each leg should be on each needle—40 sts total. 20 sts for front will be on one needle, and 20 sts for back will be on the other. Join double strand of main yarn with RS facing to the beginning of one needle. Work in Stockinette st in the rnd (round) on all 40 sts as follows:
Rnd 1: Knit the first 20 sts using both ends of the same needle, then knit the second 20 sts with both ends of the other needle.
Rnds 2 - 24: Knit in the same manner.
Rnd 25: Shape shoulders. K6, [k2tog] 2 times, [ssk] 2 times, k12, [k2tog] 2 times, [ssk] 2 times, k6—32 sts; 16 sts on each needle.
Rnds 26 - 29: Knit.
Continue according to the head directions for your chosen toy, using a double strand of main yarn.

Rabbit Head

Rnd 1: *K1, M1 (see Stitch Guide), k1; repeat from * to end of front needle, then repeat from * to end of back needle—48 sts; 24 sts on each needle.
Rnds 2 - 15: Knit.
Rnd 16: *K8, ssk, k4, k2tog, k8; repeat from * across back needle—44 sts; 22 sts on each needle.
Rnd 17: Knit.
Rnd 18: *K1, ssk, k16, k2tog, k1; repeat from * across back needle—40 sts; 20 sts on each needle.
Rnd 19: Knit.
Rnd 20: *K1, ssk, k14, k2tog, k1; repeat from * across back needle—36 sts; 18 sts on each needle.
Rnd 21: *K1, ssk, k12, k2tog, k1; repeat from * across back needle—32 sts; 16 sts on each needle.
Rnd 22: *K1, ssk, k10, k2tog, k1; repeat from * across back needle—28 sts; 14 sts on each needle.
Rnd 23: *K1, ssk, k8, k2tog, k1; repeat from * across back needle—24 sts; 12 sts on each needle.
Rnd 24: *K1, ssk, k6, k2tog, k1; repeat from * across back needle—20 sts; 10 sts on each needle.
Rnd 25: *[K2tog, k2] twice, k2tog; repeat from * across back needle—14 sts; 7 sts on each needle.

With yarn threaded on yarn needle, use Kitchener Stitch (see page 137) to graft front sts to back sts across top.

Rabbit Outer Ears (make 2)

With double strand of main yarn, cast on 16 sts. Work back and forth in rows as follows:
Row 1: (RS) Knit.
Row 2: K1, purl to last st, end k1.
Repeat these 2 rows 10 more times—22 rows completed.
Decrease Row: (RS) K1, ssk, knit to last 3 sts, k2tog, k1—2 sts decreased. Work 1 WS row as before. Repeat the last 2 rows 4 more times, then work Decrease Row once more—4 sts. Cut yarn, leaving a 12" (30.5-cm) tail. With tail threaded on a yarn needle, draw tail through remaining sts and pull snugly to close top of outer ear. Weave in ends.

Rabbit Inner Ears (make 2)

With single strand of light pink angora yarn, cast on 12 sts. Work in garter stitch (knit all sts every row) for 20 rows (10 garter ridges).
Decrease Row: (RS) K1, ssk, knit to last 3 sts, k2tog, k1—2

sts decreased. Knit 1 row. Repeat the last 2 rows 2 more times, then work Decrease Row once more—4 sts. Cut yarn, leaving a 12" (30.5-cm) tail. With tail threaded on a yarn needle, draw tail through remaining sts and pull snugly to close top of inner ear. Weave in ends.

Rabbit Ear Finishing

Lay angora inner ear on the WS (purl side) of the outer ear. With single strand of main yarn, sew inner ear to outer ear all the way around, beginning and ending at the top of the ear. The inner ear should fit just inside the edge stitches of the outer ear, and will not reach all the way to the bottom of the outer ear. Fold ear in half at bottom and sew to top of head as shown in photograph.

Finish according to general directions for all toys on page 109. Hug rabbit!

BEAR

Bear Head

Rnd 1: *K1, M1 (see Stitch Guide), k1; repeat from * to end of front needle, then repeat from * to end of back needle—48 sts; 24 sts on each needle.

Rnds 2 - 11: Knit.

Rnd 12: *K8, ssk, k4, k2tog, k8; repeat from * across back needle—44 sts; 22 sts on each needle.

Rnds 13 - 16: Knit.

Rnd 17: *K2tog, k18, ssk; repeat from * across back needle—40 sts; 20 sts on each needle. Place removable markers or safety pins in the work at each side to indicate position of the ears.

Rnds 18 - 23: Knit.

Rnd 24: *K4, ssk, k8, k2tog, k4; repeat from * across back needle—36 sts; 18 sts on each needle.

Rnds 25 - 27: Knit.

Rnd 28: *Ssk, k4, place removable marker or safety pin, ssk, k3, **transfer last st worked to left-hand needle, pass 2nd st on left-hand needle over the transferred st, return transferred st to right-hand needle,** place removable marker or safety pin, k5, repeat from ** to ** once more; repeat entire sequence from * across back needle—28 sts; 14 sts on each needle.

With yarn threaded on yarn needle, use Kitchener Stitch (see page 137) to graft front sts to back sts across top, keeping removable markers in place.

Bear Ears

Thread a single strand of the main yarn about 12" (30.5 cm) long on needle. Using markers at the top and sides of head as guides, run yarn on inside head diagonally from the top marker, down to the side ear marker, and then back up to the other top marker. Pull the ends of the yarn gently to indent the bottom of each ear to shape and define it. Tie the ends securely in a knot and pull tails to inside. Weave in ends.

Bear Scarf

With single strand of scarf yarn, cast on 8 sts. Work in garter stitch until scarf measures 14½" (37 cm) long. Bind off all sts. Weave in ends.

Finish according to general directions for all toys on page 109. Hug bear!

ELEPHANT

Elephant Head

Rnd 1: *K1, M1 (see Stitch Guide), k1; repeat from * to end— 48 sts; 24 sts on each needle.

Rnds 2 - 5: Knit.

The next few rows of the head are worked back and forth in preparation for the trunk.

Row 6: (RS) K6, k12 and place the last 12 sts on a holder, k6 to end front needle, k24 sts of back needle—36 sts on needles; 12 sts on holder at center front.

Row 7: Knit the first 6 sts of front needle, turn, and purl back across all 36 sts.

Rows 8 - 10: Keeping the sts on their same needles, work Stockinette st back and forth in rows. End having just knit the first 6 sts on the front needle on Row 10.

Resume working in the rnd on Rnd 11.

Rnd 11: Using the provisional cast-on method (see page 133), prepare a crochet chain 15 - 18 sts long. With front needle, pick up and knit 12 sts in the bumps on the back of the crochet chain, k6 to end front needle, k24 sts of back needle—48 sts; 24 sts on each needle.

Rnds 12-15: Knit

Rnd 16: *K1, ssk, k18, k2tog, k1; repeat from * across back needle—44 sts; 22 sts on each needle.

Rnd 17: Knit.

Rnd 18: *K1, ssk, k16, k2tog, k1; repeat from * across back needle—40 sts; 20 sts on each needle.

Rnd 19: Knit

Rnd 20: *K1, ssk, k14, k2tog, k1; repeat from * across back needle—36 sts; 18 sts on each needle.

Rnd 21: *K1, ssk, k12, k2tog, k1; repeat from * across back needle—32 sts; 16 sts on each needle.

Rnd 22: *K1, ssk, k10, k2tog, k1; repeat from * across back needle—28 sts; 14 sts on each needle.

Rnd 23: *K1, ssk, k8, k2tog, k1; repeat from * across back needle— 24 sts; 12 sts on each needle.

Rnd 24: *K1, ssk, k6, k2tog, k1; repeat from * across back needle—20 sts; 10 sts on each needle.

Rnd 25: *[K2tog, k2] twice, k2tog; repeat from * across back needle—14 sts; 7 sts on each needle.

With yarn threaded on yarn needle, use Kitchener Stitch (see page 137) to graft front sts to back sts across top.

Elephant Trunk

Place 12 sts from holder on dpn with RS facing. Join double strand of main yarn, and use a second dpn to pick up and knit 4 sts along side of opening, twisting the sts to close any holes. Slip the first 2 picked-up sts to the end of the first needle. Continuing with the second dpn, pick up and knit 12 sts released from the base of the provisional cast-on, then pick up and knit 4 sts along other side edge of opening. Slip the last 2 picked-up sts to end of first dpn—32 sts, 16 sts on each needle.

Rearrange sts evenly on 4 needles, and place marker to indicate beginning of rnd in the center of 4 picked-up sts from one side.

Rnd 1: *K1, ssk, k10, k2tog, k1; repeat from * to end—28 sts.
Rnd 2, 4, 6, and 8: Knit
Rnd 3: *K1, ssk, k8, k2tog, k1; repeat from * to end—24 sts.
Rnd 5: *K1, ssk, k6, k2tog, k1; repeat from * to end—20 sts.
Rnd 7: *K1, ssk, k4, k2tog, k1; repeat from * to end—16 sts.
Rnd 9: *K1, ssk, k2, k2tog, k1; repeat from * to end—12 sts.
Rnds 10 - 24: Knit.
Rnd 25: Purl.
Rnd 26: Change to a double strand of pink alpaca-silk and knit 1 rnd.
Rnd 27: K2tog around—6 sts.
Cut yarn, leaving a 12" (30.5-cm) tail. With tail threaded on a yarn needle, draw tail through remaining sts and pull snugly to close end of trunk. Take tail to inside of trunk and fasten securely. Weave in ends.

Elephant Ears (make 2)

The ears are worked back and forth in seed stitch. Pay close attention to the stitch pattern as you increase in order to keep it correct.

Using double strand of main yarn, cast on 14 sts. Work in seed st as follows:
Row 1: *K1, p1; repeat from * to end.
Row 2: (Increase Row) Kf&b (knit in front and back of st to increase 1 st), *k1, p1; repeat from * to last st, kf&b—2 sts increased.
Row 3: *P1, k1; repeat from * to end.
Repeat Rows 2 and 3 three more times—22 sts.
Knit 8 more rows in seed st.
Decrease Row: K2tog, *p1, k1; repeat from * to last 2 sts, k2tog—2 sts decreased. Work 1 row in seed st, then repeat the Decrease Row once more—18 sts. Bind off all sts in pattern. Make a pleat in the center of the cast-on edge of

each ear so the lower edge measures about 2½" (6.5 cm) wide. Using single strand of main yarn, sew the ears to the sides of the head as shown in photograph. Weave in ends.

Elephant Kerchief

With single strand of alpaca-silk pink yarn, cast on 3 sts. Work back and forth in rows as follows for 27 rows:
All Rows: Yo, knit to end—1 st increased.

At the end of 27 rows there will be 30 sts. Using the cable cast-on method (see page 132), cast on 15 sts at end of next two rows, continuing increases as set—60 sts. Bind off all sts loosely as if to knit on next row. Weave in ends.

Finish according to general directions for all toys below. Hug elephant!

Finishing (for all toys)

Cut 4 strands of main yarn 15" (38 cm) long. With 2 strands held together and beginning at left side of neck, just below increase rnd for head, weave yarn through all sts around, going over 1, under 1, and leaving ends of yarn hanging loose at the side. With the remaining 2 strands of yarn and beginning at the right side of the head, weave yarn through all sts in the next rnd below. Stuff head and neck, including elephant's trunk if applicable. Draw up each set of woven-in gathering threads to shape the neck, tie ends together, and pull ends to inside. Stuff body and legs until firm, but not lumpy, then sew remaining open seams using mattress stitch and a single strand of main yarn. Stuff arms and attach to sides of body with single strand of main yarn. Embroider eyes and mouths, if applicable, as shown in photographs. For elephant trunk, tack the underside of the trunk to front of the head so the trunk points downward as shown in photograph. Weave in any remaining ends.

MORE-THAN-EIGHT-HOUR GIFTS

HOURGLASS SWEATER

I designed this sweater to be feminine, but not fussy. I chose a wide portrait neckline and fitted raglan shaping, plus hemmed edges, waist shaping, and tapered sleeves, to create an hourglass silhouette that flatters most women's figures. The yarn is Noro's Cash Iroha, a beautiful, single-ply, handspun blend of silk, wool, and cashmere that comes in a luscious spectrum of colors and is beautifully highlighted in this simple design.

FINISHED MEASUREMENTS
Chest: 33 (37, 41, 45, 49)" (84 [94, 104, 114.5, 124.5] cm). Length from lower edge to shoulder: 21 (22, 24, 25, 25)" (53.5 [56, 61, 63.5, 63.5] cm). Sleeve length from wrist to underarm: 18½ (19½, 20, 20½, 21)" (47 [49.5, 51, 52, 53.5] cm).

YARN
Noro Cash Iroha (40% silk, 30% lambswool, 20% cashmere, 10% nylon; 100 yards [91 meters] / 40 grams): #78 orange, 10 (11, 12, 14, 15) skeins.

NEEDLES
One 32" (80-cm) circular needle size US 7 (4.5 mm).
One 12" (30-cm) circular needle size US 7 (4.5 mm).
Change needle size if necessary to obtain the correct gauge.

NOTIONS
Yarn needle, scissors, stitch markers, removable stitch markers or safety pins, stitch holders, 2 yards (2 meters) smooth cotton scrap yarn in a contrasting color (optional).

GAUGE
19 sts and 28 rows = 4" (10 cm) in Stockinette stitch.

Lower Body

With longer circular needle, cast on 79 (87, 97, 107, 117) sts for back, place marker, cast on 79 (87, 97, 107, 117) sts for front—158 (174, 194, 214, 234) sts. Join for working in the rnd (round), being careful not to twist, and place marker to indicate the beginning of the rnd. Knit 5 rnds, then purl 1 rnd for hem turning rnd. Knit 10 rnds, end last rnd 2 sts before the beginning marker.

Decrease Rnd: Ssk, k1, k2tog, knit to within 2 sts of next marker; repeat from * once more—4 sts decreased. Knit 8 (8, 10, 11, 12) rnds.

Repeat the last 9 (9, 11, 12, 13) rnds 2 more times, then work decrease rnd once more—142 (158, 178, 198, 218) sts; piece measures about 5½ (5½, 6¼, 6¾, 7)" (14 [14, 16, 17, 18] cm) above turning rnd. Work even until piece measures 6½ (6¾, 7½, 7¾, 8½)" (16.5 [17, 19, 19.5, 21.5] cm) above turning rnd, end last rnd 1 st before the beginning marker.

Increase Rnd: *Kf&b (knit into front and back of same st to increase 1 st), k1, kf&b, k to within 1 st marker repeat from * once more—4 sts increased. Knit 13 rnds.

Repeat the last 14 rnds 2 more times, then work the increase rnd once more—158 (174, 194, 214, 234) sts; piece measures about 12½ (12¾, 13½, 13¾, 14½)" (31.5 [32.5, 34.5, 35, 37] cm) above turning rnd. Work even until piece measures 15 (15, 15½, 15¾, 15)" (38 [38, 39.5, 40, 38] cm) above turning rnd.

Divide for yoke: K5, place the last 10 sts just worked on a stitch holder, knit to 5 sts beyond next marker removing marker as you go, place the last 10 sts just worked on a stitch holder, knit to end of front—69 (77, 87, 97, 107) sts each for front and back. Set aside and do not break yarn.

Sleeves (make 2)

With shorter circular needle, cast on 56 (60, 64, 68, 72) sts. Join for working in the rnd, being careful not to twist, and place marker to indicate the beginning of the rnd. Knit 5 rnds, then purl 1 rnd for hem turning rnd. Knit 10 rnds.

Decrease Rnd: K2tog, knit to last 3 sts, ssk, k1—54 (58, 62, 66, 70) sts. Knit 37 rnds, then repeat the decrease rnd once more—52 (56, 60, 64, 68) sts; piece measures about 7" (18 cm) above turning rnd. Work even until piece measures 12½" (31.5 cm) above turning rnd.

Increase Rnd: Kf&b, knit to last st, kf&b—2 sts increased. Work 16 (13, 4, 5, 5) rnds even. Repeat the last 17 (14, 5, 6, 6) rnds 1 (2, 7, 7, 8) more time(s)—56 (62, 76, 80, 86) sts. Work even until piece measures 18½ (19½, 20, 20½, 21)" (47 [49.5, 51, 52, 53.5] cm) from turning rnd. On the next rnd, k5, place the last 10 sts just worked on a stitch holder, removing the marker for end of rnd from the middle of these sts, knit to end—46 (52, 66, 70, 76) sts on needle. Break yarn.

After working the first sleeve, knit the sleeve sts onto the circular needle for the body next to the 69 (77, 87, 97, 107) sts for front, place marker, then knit the back sts. Set aside. You can then use the same needle to work the second sleeve without having to switch the first sleeve sts from needles to stitch holder and back again.

Make a second sleeve the same as the first, leaving sts on the shorter circular needle.

Yoke

Knit 46 (52, 66, 70, 76) sts from needle for left sleeve onto circular needle next to the sts for back, place marker, knit 69 (77, 87, 97, 107) sts for front—230 (258, 306, 334, 366) sts. Place marker for new beginning of rnd, which begins at front right raglan line. Use a different color marker to indicate the beginning of the rnd. Knit 1 rnd even, end last rnd 2 sts before beginning marker.

Decrease Rnd: *Ssk, k1, k2tog, knit to within 2 sts of next marker; repeat from * 3 more times—8 sts decreased, 1 plain knit st between each set of paired decrease along raglan line. Knit 1 rnd even. Repeat the last 2 rnds 15 (18, 22, 23, 25) more times—102 (106, 122, 142, 158) sts: 37 (39, 41, 49, 55) sts for front and back, and 14 (14, 20, 22, 24) sts for each sleeve. Yoke measures about 4½ (5½, 6½, 7, 7½)" (11.5 [14, 16.5, 18, 19] cm) above joining rnd.

Purl 1 rnd for neckband turning rnd. Knit 1 rnd. Increase Rnd: *Kf&b, k1, kf&b, knit to next marker: repeat from * 3 more times—8 sts increased. Repeat the last 2 rnds 2 more times—126 (130, 146, 166, 182) sts. Do not bind off.

Finishing

Before sewing down the live stitches of the neckband facing, run a piece of scrap cotton through the purl loops along the rnd of sts 6 rnds below the turning rnd; this will make it much easier to attach the live sts in a straight line to keep the neckband even. The facing of the neckband has 5 rnds beyond the turning rnd, plus the rnd represented by the sts on the needle. Count 6 rnds down on the inside below the turning rnd to find the correct rnd from which to pick up loops, then count the loops picked up on the scrap yarn. In an ideal world, there should be one loop for each live st on the needle. Typically, I find that I usually have a few too many, or a few too few. If this is the case, you can "cheat" a bit by joining 2 sts at a time from the knitting needle (if you picked up too few loops), or skipping a couple of the loops on the scrap yarn (if you picked up too many). Just make sure to space these adjustments evenly, and they should not be noticeable when you are finished.

Cut the working yarn, leaving a tail about 3 times the length of the measurement around the neck opening. Turn sweater inside out and fold the neckband to the inside along the turning rnd. Holding the neckband smoothly folded down, join the live sts on the needle to the inside of the neckline as follows: Using the tip of the threaded yarn needle, slip first st from knitting needle as if to knit, insert yarn needle tip through the marked purl bump of the st closest to the live st and pull yarn all the way through to secure. Repeat until all live sts have been joined. Cut yarn and secure last st.

Fold lower edge and sleeve facings along turning rnds and slipstitch in place. Using Kitchener stitch (see page 137), graft underarm sts together. Weave in ends.

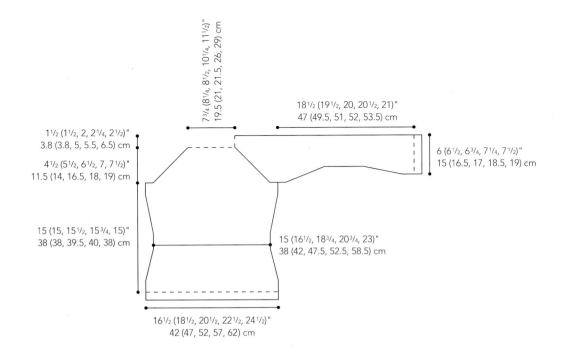

HERRINGBONE PONCHO

The poncho has made a comeback on the fashion scene, which is great news for gift knitters since this versatile garment fits just about everybody. This one is made with a wonderful blend of alpaca and merino wool that I find to be as luxurious as cashmere (but much less expensive). It is worked on large needles in order to create a warm, but not too dense, fabric that drapes beautifully.

FINISHED MEASUREMENTS
25" (63.5 cm) wide,
and 58" (147.5 cm) long,
before sewing.

YARN
Blue Sky Alpacas Worsted (50% alpaca, 50% Merino wool; 100 yards [91 meters] / 100 grams): #2003 ecru, 7 skeins.

NEEDLES
One 32" (80-cm) circular needle size US 17 (12 mm). Change needle size if necessary to obtain the correct gauge.

NOTIONS
Yarn needle, scissors, safety pins, crochet hook size P/12 (17 mm).

GAUGE
15 sts and 10½ rows = 4" (10 cm) in herringbone stitch.

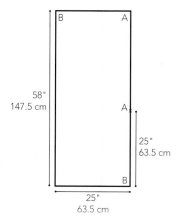

Helpful Hints:
This stitch pattern may seem a bit awkward at first, but don't worry. It becomes a lot easier as you go along. You may find it useful to hold the second stitch on the needle with your finger as you slip off the first stitch of each k2tog tbl or p2tog.

Pattern Row 1 is deliberately worked through the back loops, twisting the stitches to provide stability for the fabric. Do not be tempted to re-orient the stitches as if to work an ssk.

The stitch count of the pattern does not change. Check every few rows to make sure you have not accidentally lost a stitch, or created an extra one.

If you make a mistake, it is very simple to fix. Remove the needle from the work and slip it through the entire row of stitches below the mistake, making sure not to skip any stitches. Rip out all stitches until you come to the row that is resting on the needle, and resume knitting.

Cast on 93 sts, and work in herringbone stitch as follows:
Row 1: *K2tog tbl (through back loops) and slip only the first st off the left-hand needle, leaving second st on needle; repeat from * to end, then work k1tbl in last st on needle.
Row 2: *P2tog and slip only the first st off the left-hand needle, leaving the second st on needle; repeat from * to end, then work p1 in last st on needle.
Repeat these 2 rows until piece measures 58" (147.5 cm) from beginning. Bind off all sts as if to knit.

Finishing
Lay poncho flat with the wrong side (side with ridged horizontal welts) facing down. Mark two diagonally opposite corners at B, and mark the corner in between them A, as shown in diagram. Measure up 25" (63.5 cm) from lower right point B and place a safety pin to mark another point A. Bring both points A together and pin, then bring both points B together and pin. With crochet hook and wrong side facing, crochet slipstitch from A to B (see page 136). Fasten off last st. Weave in ends.

See page 21 for a closeup view of the stitch pattern for this poncho (the bag in the photo is sitting on the poncho).

OMBRE ALPACA BLANKET

I've always loved looking at the way the natural colors of this alpaca yarn blend into one another on the shelves at Purl. To highlight that effect, I decided to knit this blanket with two strands of yarn in different colors held together, and make a gradual transition between the stripes by changing only one color at a time. The stitch pattern I chose has a lot of depth without being too dense, and the textured surface creates "pockets" that trap warm air. This is a luxurious project that is sure to be treasured.

FINISHED MEASUREMENTS
48" (122 cm) wide, and 60½" (153.5 cm) long.

YARN
Blue Sky Alpacas Sportweight (100% alpaca; 120 yards [130 meters] / 2 ounces [57 grams]): #008 natural streaky brown (A), and #000 natural white (F), 5 skeins each; #002 natural copper (B), #003 natural medium tan (C), #004 natural light tan (D), and #005 natural taupe (E), 7 skeins each.

Yarn is used doubled throughout.

NEEDLES
One 40" (100-cm) circular needle size US 11 (8 mm). Change needle size if necessary to obtain the correct gauge.

NOTIONS
Yarn needle, scissors.

GAUGE
18 sts and 26 rows = 4" (10 cm) in pattern stitch with doubled strand of yarn.

Helpful Hint:
Count your cast-on stitches at least two times before you start knitting, and pay very close attention to your stitch pattern on the first few rows. It is very easy to get out of sync with this pattern until it has become established. Once you have worked an inch or so, the pattern will start to take shape, and you'll be able to see what you're doing; then the work will become much easier.

All slipped stitches are slipped as if to purl with yarn in back.

With 2 strands of color A, cast on 215 sts. Work in pattern as follows:
Row 1: *K1, slip 1; repeat from * to last st, k1.
Row 2: Knit.
Repeat Rows 1 and 2 until piece measures 5½" (14 cm) from beginning, ending with Row 2. Cut one strand of color A, and join 1 strand of color B. Working with 1 strand each of A and B, repeat Rows 1 and 2 until the A/B stripe measures 5½" (14 cm), and piece measures about 11" (28 cm) from beginning.

Continue in this manner, working a 5½" (14-cm) stripe in each of the following color combinations: B/B, B/C, C/C, C/D, D/D, D/E, E/E, E/F, and F/F—11 stripes completed; piece measures about 60½" (153.5 cm) from beginning.

Bind off all sts loosely as if to knit. Weave in ends.

CHEVRON SCARF

Made with contrasting colors of Koigu multicolored merino in a simple though intricate-looking stitch pattern, this scarf is a great gift for a friend who appreciates the creativity of both artisan yarn-dyeing and your own special handknitting. It does take awhile to knit, so don't start this gift too late.

FINISHED MEASUREMENTS
5" (12.5 cm) wide, and
78" (198 cm) long.

YARN
Koigu Premium Painter's
Palette Merino (KPPPM) (100%
Merino wool; 175 yards
[160 meters] / 50 grams): 2
skeins each of 2 different colors.

Shown in:
Pink/Yellow Version, #P216 (A)
and #P611 (B)
Green/Purple Version (see
page 2), #P516 (A) and #P436 (B).

NEEDLES
One set straight needles size
US 5 (3.75 mm).
Change needle size if necessary
to obtain the correct gauge.

NOTIONS
Yarn needle, scissors.

GAUGE
38 sts and 32 rows = 4" (10 cm)
in chevron pattern.

Helpful Hint:
When switching between the two colors, pick up the new color in front of the old color every time. This way the yarns will be carried neatly along the edge of the scarf as you knit.

With color A, cast on 48 sts. Starting with a purl row, work 4 rows reverse Stockinette stitch (purl all sts on RS rows, knit all sts on WS rows), beginning with a RS purl row. Work in chevron pattern as follows:

Row 1: (RS) Change to B. [K2tog] 4 times,* [kf&b] 8 times, [k2tog] 8 times; rep from *, ending last repeat [k2tog] 4 times.
Row 2: Purl.
Row 3: Change to A and knit.
Row 4: Purl.

Repeat these 4 rows until piece measures 77½" (197 cm), or until there is just enough yarn left to work 4 more rows and bind off, ending with Row 2. Change to A and work 4 rows reverse Stockinette stitch, beginning with a RS purl row.

Bind off all sts loosely. Weave in ends.

The model is wearing one scarf, which is wrapped around her head and then neck, with enough length left over to drape elegantly in front.

MEN'S ZIPPED RAGLAN

Handknit sweaters for men present a constant challenge. Not only are men hard to design for, their sweaters can be so big that they take forever to finish! This sweater is knit using a chunky wool and is made in one piece, in order to keep the knitting moving quickly. The red zipper, a modern touch, provides an element of color and fun while still keeping the sweater looking masculine. It also gives a man the option of wearing the sweater open if he's the type that gets hot easily.

FINISHED MEASUREMENTS
Chest: 39½ (42, 46½, 51)" (100.5 [106.5, 118, 129.5] cm). Length from lower edge to shoulder: 24 (25, 26, 27)" (61 [63.5, 66, 68.5] cm). Sleeve length from wrist to underarm: 18½ (19, 20, 21)" (47 [48.5, 51, 53.5] cm).

YARN
Manos del Uruguay (100% handspun kettle-dyed wool; 137 yards [125 meters] / 100 grams): #37 thrush (dark brown), 8 (9, 10, 11) skeins.

NEEDLES
One 40" (100-cm) circular needle size US 9 (5.5 mm). One 24" (60-cm) circular needle size US 9 (5.5 mm). One 16" (40-cm) circular needle size US 9 (5.5 mm). Change needle size if necessary to obtain the correct gauge.

NOTIONS
Yarn needle, scissors, stitch markers, removable stitch markers or safety pins, stitch holders, red plastic separating zipper 25 (26, 27, 28)" (63.5 [66, 68.5, 71] cm) long, sharp-pointed sewing needle, thread to match zipper, sewing pins.

GAUGE
14½ sts and 22 rows = 4" (10 cm) in k4, p4 rib, lightly blocked.

With longest circular needle, cast on 38 (40, 44, 48) sts for left front, pm (place marker), cast on 72 (76, 84, 92) sts for back, pm, cast on 38 (40, 44, 48) sts for right front—148 (156, 172, 188) sts. Do not join for working in the rnd (round). Working back and forth in rows, establish k4, p4 rib pattern with k1, p1 rib at center fronts as follows:
Row 1: (RS) [K1, p1] 2 times, *k4, p4; repeat from * to last 8 sts, end k4, [p1, k1] 2 times.
Row 2: [P1, k1] 2 times, p4, *k4, p4; repeat from * to last 4 sts, end [k1, p1] 2 times.
Repeat these 2 rows until piece measures 15 (15½, 16½, 16¾)" (38 [39.5, 41.5, 42.5] cm) from beginning, ending with a RS (right side) row.

Divide for yoke: On the next WS row, work in pattern to 4 sts past the first m (marker) and removing m as you go, place the last 8 sts just worked on a stitch holder, work in pattern to 4 sts beyond next m removing marker as you go, place the last 8 sts just worked on a stitch holder, work in pattern to end—34 (36, 40, 44) sts for each front, 64 (68, 76, 84) sts for back. Turn, and work 34 (36, 40, 44) sts for right front only. Set aside and do not break yarn.

Sleeves (make 2)
With shortest circular needle, cast on 48 sts. Join for working in the rnd, being careful not to twist, and pm to indicate the beginning of the rnd. Establish k4, p4 rib pattern as follows: P2, *k4, p4; repeat from * to last 6 sts, end k4, p2. Work in rib pattern for a total of 16 rnds—piece measures about 3" (7.5 cm) from beginning. Increase Rnd: Kf&b, knit to last st, kf&b—2 sts increased. Work increased sts into the k4, p4 rib pattern as they become available, changing to the medium length circular needle if there are too many sts to fit comfortably on the shortest circular needle. Work 8 (7, 7, 6) rnds even. Repeat the last 9 (8, 8, 7) rnds 8 (9, 10, 11) more times—66 (68, 70, 72) sts. Work even until piece measures 18½ (19, 20, 21)" (47 [48.5, 51, 53.5] cm) from beginning. On the next rnd, work 4 sts in pattern, place the last 8 sts just worked on a stitch holder, removing the m for end of rnd from the middle of these sts, work in pattern to end—58 (60, 62, 64) sts on needle. Break yarn.

After working the first sleeve, work the sleeve sts onto the end of the longer circular needle for the body holding the right front sts, pm, work the back sts,

pm. Then you can use the same shorter circular needle to make the second sleeve without having to switch the first sleeve sts from needles to stitch holder and back again.

Make a second sleeve the same as the first, leaving sts on the shorter circular needle.

Yoke

Work the sts for the left sleeve onto the end of the circular needle holding the sts for the back, pm, then work across left front sts to end—248 (260, 280, 300) sts. Work 1 WS row, working all sts as they appear.

Note: Throughout the raglan decreasing 2 knit sts will be maintained on either side of the marked raglan line when viewed from the RS.
Decrease Row: (RS) On right front work in pattern to 3 sts before m, k2tog, k1, sl m, on right sleeve *k1, ssk, work in pattern to 3 sts before next m, k2tog, k1, sl m; repeat from * 2 more times for sts on back and left sleeve, then on left front k1, ssk, work in rib pattern to end—8 sts decreased. Work 1 row even on WS. Repeat the last 2 rows 18 (19, 20, 21) more times, changing to the medium length circular needle, if desired, as the number of sts decreases—96 (100, 112, 124) sts: 15 (16, 19, 22) sts for each front, 20 sts for each sleeve, 26 (28, 34, 40) sts for back. Sleeves Only Decrease Row: (RS) Work even across right front sts, sl m, on right sleeve k1, ssk, work in pattern to 3 sts before m, k2tog, k1, work even across back sts, sl m, on left sleeve k1, ssk, work in pattern to 3 sts before m, k2tog, k1, sl m, work even across left front sts—4 sts decreased, 2 sts from each sleeve. Work 1 row even on wrong side. Repeat the last 2 rows 2 more times—84 (88, 100, 112) sts: 15 (16, 19, 22) sts for each front, 14 sts for each sleeve, 26 (28, 34, 40) sts for back; piece measures about 7 (7½, 7¾, 8¼)" (18 [19, 19.5, 21] cm) above joining row. Mark each side of the last row with a removable marker or safety pin to indicate the base of the collar.

Collar

Continue to work even in pattern until collar measures 3½" (9 cm) above markers for base of collar, ending with a RS row. Knit across all sts on the next row (WS) to form a turning row. Resume rib pattern, and work until collar measures 3½" (9 cm) above the turning row. Bind off all sts loosely in pattern.

Finishing

Using Kitchener stitch (see page 137), graft underarm sts together. Weave in ends. Close zipper and pin in place along center front opening with the top of the zipper even with the turning row of the collar. Using sewing needle and thread, sew zipper to fronts along the valley of the first purl st in from the center front edge, being careful to keep the two fronts even, and aligning the edge of the garment with the base of the zipper teeth. Fold collar to inside along turning row. With yarn threaded on a yarn needle, sew bound-off edge of collar to inside of sweater. With sewing needle and thread, sew front edges of collar facing to zipper tape, in line with the base of the zipper teeth. Block lightly, if desired, to flatten and slightly reduce the corrugated effect of the rib pattern.

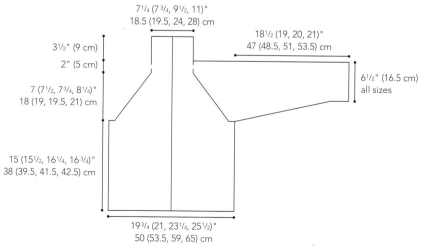

7 1/4 (7 3/4, 9 1/2, 11)"
18.5 (19.5, 24, 28) cm

18 1/2 (19, 20, 21)"
47 (48.5, 51, 53.5) cm

3 1/2" (9 cm)

2" (5 cm)

6 1/2" (16.5 cm)
all sizes

7 (7 1/2, 7 3/4, 8 1/4)"
18 (19, 19.5, 21) cm

15 (15 1/2, 16 1/4, 16 3/4)"
38 (39.5, 41.5, 42.5) cm

19 3/4 (21, 23 1/4, 25 1/2)"
50 (53.5, 59, 65) cm

WRAPPING HANDKNIT GIFTS

After putting so much time and thought into creating a handknit gift it's nice to wrap it in such a way that the recipient knows right away that he or she is getting something special and unique. However, having spent time making a gift, we don't always have time to labor over the wrapping. Here are some simple ideas I like to use.

Tissue Paper

One of the simplest ways to present a handknit gift is wrapped—without a box—in colored tissue paper in a beautiful color that complements the gift. It doesn't really matter if the paper is slightly wrinkled, or if the corners are perfectly square. I like to tie the package with yarn leftover from the project and to make a gift tag or card by stamping the recipient's name on a pretty piece of paper. I think this wrapping has a sweet, imperfect feeling just like many handmade gifts.

Woven Box

If you give a handknit gift inside a woven box, you don't have to spend any time wrapping it and the recipient always has a special and safe place to store it. I like to use woven boxes in colors that contrast with the project colors. Look for woven boxes at stationery and craft supply stores.

Soft Drawstring Pouch

The Soft Drawstring Pouch (see pattern on page 84) can serve as a wrapping for another handknit or, if the recipient is also a knitter, a couple of skeins of beautiful yarn.

Indian Cotton Bag with Twisted Cord Drawstring

I love Indian cotton because it feels nice, comes in a spectrum of wonderful colors, and is inexpensive. A bag made from Indian cotton—like a woven box—doubles as a wrapping and as a safe-storage container. To make a bag, cut a length of fabric 12" (30 cm) wide x 33" (84 cm) long. Fold the fabric in half lengthwise, sew one seam up each side leaving a ½" (1.3 cm) seam allowance. Turn the open end of the bag ½" (1.3 cm) to the wrong side, sew across each side to make channels for the drawstrings. Turn right side out, pull cord through each half of the channel using a safety pin. The drawstrings on the bag shown in the photo are made with a twisted cord (see directions below) out of pure silk yarn called La Luz from Fiesta Yarns. Indian cotton can be purchased at most fine fabric stores.

Twisted Cords

I like to use twisted cord as "ribbon" on boxes and as drawstrings on bags. To make a twisted cord, cut a long length of yarn, about a third more than double the length you will need to wrap your package. Tie one end of the length around something steady, such as a doorknob. Twist the other end with the twist of the plies until the yarn tries to coil up on itself. Using your free hand grasp the center of the length and bring the free end of the yarn to the doorknob end and tie them together. Let the cord twist by itself. If desired, embellish the ends of the cords with pompoms.

Pompoms

For creative pompom-making, see page 42.

Minis

The Sweater and Stocking Minis (see page 46) make sweet details on packages and can then be used by the recipient as decorations.

Yarn Ribbon

It's often effective to use multiple strands of yarn leftover from a gift project as ribbon. Or, if you're giving a felted gift, make an I-cord "ribbon" with the gift yarn and felt it along with the rest of the project. To wrap the felted potholders shown here (see instructions on page 49), I felted 120" (3 meters) of 3-stitch I-cord (made from leftover Manos del Uruguay wool); the cord shrunk about 30% in length during felting.

Tassels

Tassels look great on packages and can be kept by the recipient to be used as ornaments or lamp pulls. The tassel shown here is made the same way and with the same yarn as the tassel on page 40, but the neck is finished with a spiral-cord macrame knot.

To make the spiral-cord neck on the tassel, you must first secure the tassel to something vertically, with the head at the top so that you can use both hands while working the knots. One way to do this is to safety pin it to something stable that won't be damaged by the pin. This tassel was pinned to the knee of a pair of jeans that the knitter was wearing. Cut a length of yarn about 20 inches (51 cm), place the strand horizontally under the tassel at the point where you want the top of the neck to begin (ours is ¾" [1.9 cm] down) and tie once. *Wrap the right side of the strand around the back of the tassel, leaving a loop on the right side of the tassel that looks like a backwards "c" and over the top of the left-hand strand. Pick up the left-hand strand over the top of the right-hand strand, then through the backwards "c" of the right-hand strand, pull both strands equally to tighten the knot. Repeat from * for 2 inches (5 cm), tie off, trim ends to match end of tassel.

For the package shown here, I ran a long crocheted chain through the head of the tassel, securing the tassel at the center point by making a square knot in the chain. I then wrapped the chain around the package. This makes the box look very elegant even though it is only wrapped in plain tissue paper.

FINAL FLOURISH

As a final, thoughtful flourish, I like to complete a gift with a neatly written card explaining how to care for the gift; a bit of extra yarn and an extra button, if necessary; and a sachet filled with lavender or fresh cedar balls to keep bugs away.

SPECIAL TECHNIQUES

The techniques shown here are used in the projects in this book.

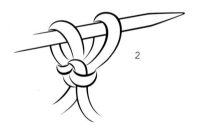

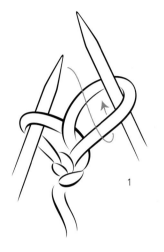

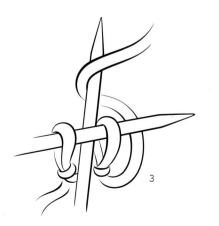

Cable Cast-On

A cable cast-on creates a flexible edge which is great when you are working cables. It is also a convenient way to cast-on extra stitches at the end of a row. When you know that you'll want to pick up stitches along the cast-on edge when you are finishing your work, the cable cast-on is very handy because it makes small, easily distinguishable loops along the cast-on edge.

Make a slipknot and place it on your left-hand needle. Using your right-hand needle, knit into this stitch, wrap yarn around the right-hand needle as you normally would when knitting, and pull a loop of yarn through the slipknot (as shown in illustration 1). Slip the point of the left-hand needle into the back of the stitch on the right-hand needle, and transfer the stitch onto left-hand needle; you now have two stitches on the left-hand needle (as shown in illustration 2). Next, *slip the point of the right-hand needle between the two stitches on the left-hand needle, wrap yarn as you normally would when knitting (as shown in illustration 3), and pull up a loop of yarn from between the stitches. Slip the point of the left-hand needle into the back of the stitch on the right-hand needle, and transfer the stitch onto the left-hand needle. Repeat from * until the correct number of stitches have been cast-on.

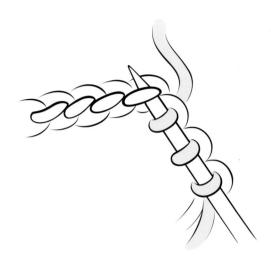

Provisional Cast-On

Use a piece of cotton waste yarn in a contrasting color but similar weight to the yarn you are working with. Crochet a chain three or four stitches longer than the number of stitches you need to cast on, then cut the yarn and pull the tail through the last chain stitch to fasten off. If you examine the back of the crochet chain, you will see that its underside has a row of bumps. Pick up and knit one stitch in each of these bumps until you have the correct amount of stitches for your cast-on. When you need to pick up stitches from the provisional cast-on edge again, undo the tail of the crochet chain, and gently "unzip" the chain to release the stitches, carefully transferring each stitch to a needle as it becomes free.

Three-Needle Bind-Off

With the wrong side of each piece of fabric facing out, and the needles parallel, slip a third (working) needle into the first stitch on each of the other two needles. Wrap yarn around working needle as if to knit, and pull a loop through. Allow the first stitch from each of the parallel needles to fall from the needles. *Knit together the new first stitch on both parallel needles in the same way; there will be two stitches on the working needle. Using one of the two parallel needles, pass the first stitch on the working needle over the second stitch and off the needle as you normally would when binding off. Repeat from * until only one stitch remains on the working needle. Break yarn and pull the tail through the last stitch to fasten off.

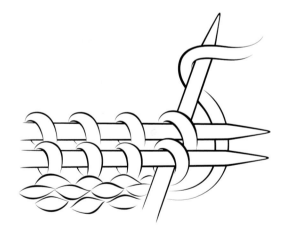

Mattress Stitch

Lay the pieces to be sewn together right side up. Thread a yarn needle with the same yarn used to knit your piece. Insert the yarn needle into the first piece of fabric in the very first row of knitting, between the edge stitch and the second stitch, to the back of the piece. Pass the needle under one strand of the fabric, then bring the needle to the front again. Insert the needle into the very first row of the other piece of fabric, again between the edge stitch and the second stitch, bring the needle to the front of the fabric again, and pull gently. The two pieces have now been joined for the beginning of the mattress stitch seam.

Insert the yarn needle into the first piece of fabric between the edge stitch and the second stitch in the first row of knitting. Pass the needle underneath the two horizontal bars connecting the edge stitch to the second stitch, and bring the needle back to the front of the fabric. Next, *pass the yarn needle into the same hole where the yarn exited on the opposite piece of fabric, and slip the yarn needle underneath the two horizontal bars connecting the edge stitch and the second stitch, and bring the needle back to the front of the fabric. Repeat from * several times, then pull the yarn gently to bring the two halves of the seam together, being careful not to pull too tightly and pucker the seam, then continue until the seam is fully sewn.

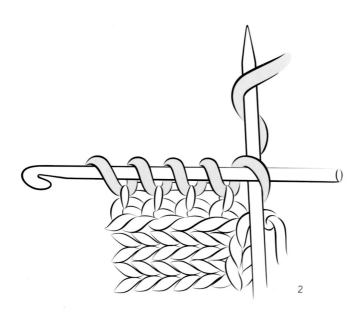

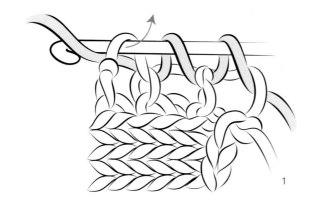

Picking Up Stitches

Some knitters work this technique with a knitting needle, but I prefer to use a crochet hook because it doesn't seem to stretch out the edge stitches quite as much.

Lay the work right side up with the edge you will be picking up at the top. Pull a tail from the yarn you will be using to pick up that is about 3 times the length of the edge. When you pick up these stitches you will be picking up loops with the tail, and then later knitting the same loops with the working end of the yarn. I find it helpful to lay the tail parallel to the edge starting at the right and ending at the left. Insert the crochet hook into the first row of knitting between the loop made by the edge stitch and the first stitch, wrap yarn over hook and pull a loop through. *Insert crochet hook into the next row of knitting between the loop made by the edge stitch and the first stitch, wrap yarn over hook and pull a loop through. Repeat from * until you have about 8 to 10 loops on your crochet hook (see illustration 1). Slide loops to the opposite end of the crochet hook, and knit them off onto your right-hand needle using the working end of the yarn (see illustration 2). Resume picking up loops, knitting them off the handle of the crochet hook as you go, until all the picked up loops have been knit.

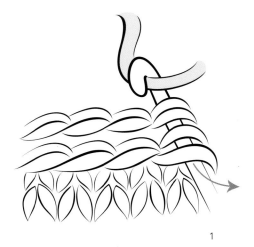

1

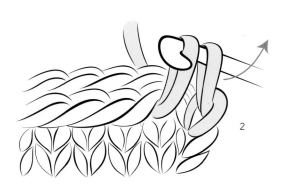

2

Crochet Slip Stitch

The illustration and directions for this are specifically for finishing the Gusseted Floor Cushions found on page 86, but you can use a slip stitch anywhere, even for decoration. The cushions use the slip stitch to join two layers of knitted fabric together. Sometimes you might want to use a slip stitch on a single layer of fabric to finish or otherwise decorate the edge.

Hold the two pieces of fabric together, with wrong sides touching and right sides facing outward (on the cushions the knit side is the wrong side and the purl side is the right side). Insert the crochet hook underneath the first bound-off stitch of the piece closest to you, and then underneath the first bound-off stitch of the second piece, as shown, making sure to insert the hook under both legs of each stitch (see illustration 1). Draw up a loop. *Insert the crochet hook underneath the next bound-off stitch for both pieces, draw up a loop, and immediately draw the new loop through the loop on the hook (see illustration 2). Repeat from * until all stitches have been joined. Break yarn and pull the tail through the last stitch on the hook to fasten off.

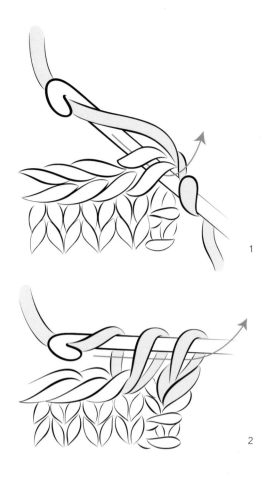

1

2

Single Crochet Edge

Begin by placing a slipknot onto the crochet hook. *Insert the crochet hook through the edge of the knitted fabric (see illustration 1). Wrap the yarn over the hook and pull a loop of yarn through the knitted fabric (2 loops on crochet hook). Wrap the yarn over the hook again and pull a loop of yarn through both loops; one loop remains on the hook (see illustration 2). Repeat from *. When you are going around corners, work 3 or 4 stitches into the same corner stitch of the knitted fabric.

Kitchener Stitch

Ktitchener stitch is a wonderful technique for weaving together live stitches using a yarn needle. I did not include an illustration for this technique because I have found that many people become confused when they see Kitchener stitch illustrated but learn quickly when they read a written description of it.

Thread a yarn needle with the same yarn used to knit your piece. Hold the two pieces of knitting, right sides out, so that the needles are parallel.

Set up stitches:
Insert the yarn needle into the first stitch on the front knitting needle as if to purl, leave stitch on knitting needle, pull yarn through.

Insert yarn needle into the first stitch on back knitting needle as if to knit, leave stitch on knitting needle, pull yarn through.

Repeat stitches:
*Insert yarn needle into the first stitch on front knitting needle as if to knit and slip stitch off of knitting needle, pull yarn through.

Insert yarn needle into next stitch on front knitting needle as if to purl, and leave stitch on knitting needle, pull yarn through.

Insert yarn needle into first stitch on back knitting needle as if to purl, slip stitch from knitting needle, pull yarn through.

Insert yarn needle in the next stitch on the back knitting needle as if to knit, leave stitch on back knitting needle,

Repeat from * until no stitches remain.

RECOMMENDED READING

Here is a list of my favorite books.

HOW-TO

How to Knit, Debbie Bliss
(Trafalgar Square)
This is one of the best reference books around, especially for beginners. The instructions are presented clearly and simply with large illustrations. Each chapter introduces a new skill. This book also has patterns; even if you don't want to knit the patterns, the instructional value of this title is priceless.

Vogue Knitting: The Ultimate Knitting Book, The Editors of Vogue Knitting Magazine (Sixth & Spring Books)
This book is often held up as the ultimate knitting guide, and in many ways it is. It has tons of detailed information as well as a catalog of design techniques. I don't always recommend this book for beginners because the sheer amount of material can be overwhelming.

Kids Knitting, Melanie Falick (Artisan)
Meant to teach children to knit, this book also happens to be an excellent resource for adults!

Hand Knitting: New Directions, Alison Ellen (Crowood Press)
A gorgeous book full of techniques for all skill levels, including an explanation of how stitches work and sections on design and working with color. It also includes patterns for sweaters, coats, hats, and other accessories.

A Treasury of Knitting Patterns, Volumes 1 – 4, Barbara Walker (Schoolhouse Press)
These four volumes contain over 1,000 different stitch patterns, including textured knit-purl combinations, slip-stitch texture and color patterns, mosaic patterns, cables, lace, eyelets, and borders. The most comprehensive collection of stitch patterns available.

A Compendium of Finishing Techniques, Naomi McEneely (Interweave Press)
A thorough, illustrated reference for finishing techniques used for knitting, weaving, sewing, and quilting.

The Knitter's Companion, Vicki Square (Interweave Press)
This small, spiral-bound book (designed to fit in your knitting bag) explains and illustrates the most-used knitting techniques.

BABIES & CHILDREN

Knitting for Baby,
Melanie Falick and Kristin Nicholas (Stewart, Tabori & Chang)
This is a great learn-to-knit book with patterns for babies and toddlers. It is filled with detailed, illustrated instructions, plus patterns for blankets, sweaters, hats, booties, and toys for baby, plus a mother's sweater and a felted diaper bag. Most of the projects are beginner and intermediate level; many will hold the attention of more experienced knitters as well.

Baby Knits for Beginners, Debbie Bliss (Trafalgar Square)
Another excellent book for soon-to-be mothers, particularly those who don't yet know how to knit. It includes great designs, with each technique explained and clearly illustrated in the pattern itself.

Simple Knits for Cherished Babies, Erika Knight (Collins & Brown)
A lovely collection of patterns for babies from newborn to nine months. Each pattern is simple, elegant, and relatively quick to knit. Choices include sweaters, a hat, leggings, blankets, toys, pillows, and booties.

ADULTS & OTHER

Knitters Almanac, Elizabeth Zimmermann (Dover Publications)
This book contains 12 patterns (some have a few variations), one for each month of the year. The patterns in this book are wonderful "old-fashioned" classics.

Weekend Knitting, Melanie Falick (Stewart, Tabori & Chang)
A diverse collection of contemporary patterns for the home, adults, and children. The poncho pattern is one of my all-time favorites.

Felted Knits, Beverly Galeskas (Interweave Press)
From a true felting expert, thirty-six designs (including bags, totes, hats, mittens, slippers, pillows, placemats, and

coasters), plus indispensable guidelines for choosing yarn for felting, and sizing and caring for felted projects.

DESIGNING YOUR OWN PATTERNS

Knitting Without Tears,
Elizabeth Zimmermann
(Simon & Schuster)
All of Elizabeth Zimmermann's books are wonderful, witty, and wry. Zimmermann teaches knitters how to develop their own designs and techniques (her term for this is "unventions"). She also gives instructions for many of her own innovative designs and unventions. This is the quintessential title from Elizabeth Zimmerman. It has excellent information for creating several different styles of seamless sweaters, and a few other projects in the round.

Knitting Around,
Elizabeth Zimmermann
(Schoolhouse Press)
This book is full of patterns and unventions as well as Elizabeth Zimmermann's fascinating autobiography. The Bog Jacket is one of my favorites.

Knitting Workshop,
Elizabeth Zimmermann
(Schoolhouse Press)
A companion to Elizabeth Zimmermann's television series, "The Busy Knitter," and "The Busy Knitter II." Both series are available on VHS from Schoolhouse Press. It is filled with techniques for hats, seamless sweaters, color knitting, and other wonderful things.

Knitting in the Nordic Tradition,
Vibeke Lind (Lark Books)
An amazing collection of traditional Norwegian knitting patterns. Although some of the projects can feel too "Old World" for some knitters, many are old enough to be new again. This is a great book to learn from when you want to create your own designs.

The Sweater Workshop,
Jacqueline Fee (Down East Books)
This books draws upon the techniques of Elizabeth Zimmermann but goes into more detail. It's great if you're looking to design your own sweaters in the round.

The Knitter's Handy Book of Patterns,
Ann Budd (Interweave Press)
A fantastic book of basic designs for sweaters, hats, mittens, and gloves in multiple sizes and gauges. If you're having trouble finding a classic unembellished pattern to work with your favorite yarn, this is the book for you.

COLOR AND FIBER

Color Works, The Crafter's Guide to Color, Deb Menz (Interweave Press)
Through photos of different color palettes with explanations of how the colors interact in fiber, plus a pull-out color wheel, and perforated color chips, this book provides readers with both a theoretical and hands-on look at color theory.

Color and Fiber, P. Lambert,
B. Staepelaere, M. Fry
(Schiffer Publishing Ltd.)
An in-depth exploration of color theory and practical information about working with color in fiber. Although it focuses primarily on color in weaving, this book is still invaluable.

Interaction of Color, Josef Albers
(Yale University Press)
This is probably the most influential book about color ever written. It is not a didactic explanation of color theories; rather, it shows readers how to discover new ways of working with color. It will encourage you to see color in a whole new light.

In Sheep's Clothing, Nola and Jane Fournier (Interweave Press)
A guide to different breeds of sheep and the unique characteristics of their wool. Aimed at handspinners, it is a wonderful resource for anyone interested in learning about the fibers with which they work.

INSPIRATION

Unexpected Knitting, Debbie New
(Schoolhouse Press)
One of the most inspirational knitting books I've ever seen. It includes detailed and comprehensive patterns for projects made from freeform knitting, scribble lace, swirl knitting, labyrinth knitting, and many more extraordinary and innovative techniques.

The Joy of Knitting, Lisa Myers
(Running Press Book Publishers)
This is a wonderful book about the knitting experience written by a yarn shop owner. Topics covered include everything from yarn selection, to gifts, to the knitting community. Each of the twelve chapters concludes with a pattern. There is also a short section on knitting basics.

Knitwear in Fashion, Sandy Black
(Thames & Hudson)
Although this book doesn't contain any patterns, it features an amazing collection of knitted garments, sculpture, jewelry, bags, and furnishings that will inspire you to push your knitting in new and exciting directions. Designers represented include Prada, Missoni, Issey Miyake, Jean Paul Gaultier and Azzedine Alaia, among many others.

SOURCES FOR SUPPLIES

All yarn and knitting supplies featured in this book are available from:

PURL
137 Sullivan St.
New York, NY 10012
212 420 8796
www.purlsoho.com

To find a local source for the yarn and other supplies featured in this book, contact the distributors below:

ANNY BLATT
7796 Boardwalk
Brighton, MI 48116
248 486 6160

BAABAJOES
PO Box 260604
Lakewood, Colorado 80226
888 222 5553
www.baabajoeswool.com

CASCADE YARNS
PO Box 58168
Tukwila, WA 98138
800 548 1048
www.cascadeyarns.com

BLUE SKY ALPACAS
P.O. Box 387
St. Francis, MN 55050
888 460 8862
www.blueskyalpacas.com

CLASSIC ELITE YARNS
300A Jackson St.
Lowell, MA 01852
800 343 0308
www.classiceliteyarns.com

FIESTA YARNS
4583 Corrales Rd.
Corrales, NM 87048
505 892 5008

KNITTING FEVER INC.
35 Debevoise Ave.
PO Box 502
Roosevelt NY 11575
516 546 3600

JOSEPH GALLER
Imported Yarns
5 Mercury Ave.
Monroe, NY 10950
845 783 3381

KOIGU WOOL DESIGNS
RR #1
Willamsford, ON
NOH 2VO, Canada
519 794 3066
www.koigu.com

LOUET SALES
808 Commerce Park Dr.
Ogdensburg, NY 13669
631 925 4502
www.louet.com

MANOS DEL URUGUAY
PO Box 770
Medford, MA 02180
888 566 9970

MISSION FALLS
Unique Kolours
28 North Bacton Hill Rd.
Malvern, PA 19335
610 280 7720
www.uniquekolours.com

MUENCH YARNS, GGH
285 Bel Marin Keys Blvd.,
  Unit J
Novato, CA 94949
800 733 9276
www.muenchyarns.com

ROWAN YARNS
Westminster Fibers
4 Townsend West, Unit 8
Nashua, NH 03063
603 886 5041
wfibers@aol.com
OTHER SUPPLIES:

Pages 18, 25 & 27
Needle Cases
Made exclusively for **Purl**
  by Etui
available from **Purl** (see left)

Page 21
Yarn shown in soft
  drawstring pouch
100% Handspun Cashmere
Coastal Cashmere Co.
HandSpun Yarns
by Hatie Clingerman
574 Davis Rd.
Union, ME 04862
207 785 5633

Page 27
Accessories & Tools
Clover Shiro measuring tape
Clover flower head blocking
  pins
Skacel needle gauge
Clover bent-tip tapestry needle
Clover point protectors, small
Yarn Craft Supply cable needle
Mondial Embroidery scissor
Boye crochet hook
Clover split ring markers
Clover ring markers, small and
  large
Clover yarn bobbin
Yarn Craft Supply stitch hold-
  ers, small & large
Yarn Craft Supply row counter,
  small
All available from Purl (see left)
  and most fine knitting shops

Page 46
Handmade paper notecards
New York Central
Art Supply
62 3rd Ave.
New York, NY 10003
800 950 6111
www.nycentralart.com

Page 73
Giraffe note card
Kate's Paperie
561 Broadway
New York, NY 10012
212 941 9816
www.katespaperie.com

Page 73
Green glass beads (used
  for buttons)
Leekan Designs
93 Mercer St.
New York, NY 10012
212 226 7226
www.leekandesigns.com

Page 79
Blue gift box
Kate's Paperie
(see above)

Page 87
Foam for gusseted floor
  cushions
4" x 18" x 18"
XL Polyurathane foam form
Canal Rubber & Supply
329 Canal St.
New York, NY 10013
 212 226 7339

Page 126
Lavender gift card
Letter stamps and ink
Tissue paper
All from Kate's Paperie
(see above)

Page 128
Green woven gift box
Orange gift card with envelope
Both from **Kate's Paperie**
(see above)

Page 129
Indian Cotton
B&J Fabrics
525 7th Ave., 2nd fl.
New York, NY 10018
212 354 8150

Page 129
Dried Lavender
Erbe
196 Prince St.
New York, NY 10012
212 966 1445

INDEX

ACKNOWLEDGMENTS

Of all the things I have ever dreamed of doing in my life, writing has never been among them. This book would not have been possible without the enormous contribution of my editor, Melanie Falick. She not only came up with the concept for this book, she took my sometimes overly complicated writing and clarified it, setting my ideas free. Her comments and suggestions allowed me to express something I am very proud of. The beautiful photographs you see here were created by Anna Williams, a dear friend whose work I have known, loved, and been influenced by for a long time. I am honored to have worked with her on this project. Asya Palatova, a friend as well as an accomplished ceramist, contributed her outstanding graphic design skills to pull all of the different elements together in a vibrant and beautiful format. Although I've never met technical editor Lori Gayle in person, I was thrilled to place my patterns in her care.

Many of the ideas in this book were inspired by projects created by customers at Purl. The Angora Baby Booties and Baby's Denim Drawstring Pants were inspired by similar projects made by Sydney Albertini for her son. The Chevron Scarf was inspired by a dazzling scarf Susan Jacobs wore into Purl one day. The Lovable Toys were inspired by the Rare Bear, a garter-stitch teddy bear created by Marion Edmonds and Ahza Moore of Knitting Together NYC. They developed the patterns for the teddy, rabbit, and elephant based on my ideas, but ultimately, they created toys that far exceeded my expectations. The Mini Sweater was originally created by Ahza Moore for sale as a Christmas ornament at Purl, and I am pleased that she allowed me to include it in this book along with her Mini Stocking.

I had been thinking about the Felted Yoga Mat Bag for a long time, but I knew I wouldn't be able to make it in time for the photo shoot without some help. I am grateful to Beverly Galeskas, the Fiber Trends felting guru, who developed the pattern and created the tote for me. Kim Hamlin, a gifted and remarkable young woman, created Kim's Hats and the Children's Cotton Hats and also found the stitch pattern for the Herringbone Poncho. Kim also knitted many of the samples, modeled for photos, and ran Purl while I was at home writing and rewriting, knitting and reknitting. Mary Lou Risely took my sketchy, half-baked idea and created the elegantly constructed, beautiful Cabled Purse; she also knitted samples for photography.

How can I ever truly thank Kelly McKaig, who flew in to New York from Chicago, stayed up until the wee hours of the morning, knitted, propped, modeled, and helped me to style this book? Without Kelly looking over my shoulder I never would have completed *Last-Minute Knitted Gifts*. Jennifer Hoverson, my sister, business partner, and best friend, happily knitted for hours on end during her New York vacation, and also displayed enormous patience with my singular focus on this book while she worked to get Purl's website, purlsoho.com, off the ground. Sasha Rockwell eagerly knitted both of the Chevron Scarves during her summer vacation in France, completed the Angora Baby Booties in one night from a very rough first draft of the pattern, and modeled. Brenda Overstrom, who teaches knitting classes at Purl, came up with the ideas for and knitted both the Pashmina Cowl and the Airy Scarf while her children were home from college for Thanksgiving.

Several other friends put their apprehensions aside and agreed to model: Charles Dort, Alexia Lewnes, Molly Montana Schnick, Jennifer Coard, Barbara Nagle, Burcu Avsar, Finn Antonson, David Mehr, and Jay Silver. Also modeling are The Desanto Family, Morgan Ackerman, and Maya Butters and her beautiful daughter. When I look through the photos and see all of these wonderful friends, both old and new, I feel blessed and thankful for their generosity.

In the end I was able to dedicate myself to working on *Last-Minute Knitted Gifts* because of the confidence I have in my amazing employees at Purl: Kim Hamlin, Molly Montana Schnick, Faye Rubenstein, Isabelle Grizzard, Sasha Rockwell, and Brenda Overstrom.